Sahib Sadhu

The White Sadhu

साहिब साधू

Sushil Choudhury,
Shree Maa and Devotees

Published by

Devi Mandir Publications

साहिब साधू

Sahib Sadhu The White Sadhu
First Edition, Copyright © 2001
by Devi Mandir Publications
5950 Highway 128
Napa, CA 94558 USA
Communications: Phone and Fax 1-707-966-2802
E-Mail swamiji@shreemaa.org
Please visit us on the World Wide Web at
http://www.shreemaa.org/

ISBN 1-877795-49-6
Library of Congress Catalog Card Number
CIP 2001 126188

Sahib Sadhu The White Sadhu
Choudhury, Sushil; Maa, Shree
1. Hindu Religion. 2. Biography. 3. Spirituality.
4. Philosophy. I. Maa, Shree;
Choudhury, Sushil

Table of Contents

Sushil's Stories

Sahib Sadhu

He arrived in our village in the dusty interior of West Bengal one day in the summer of 1970. He looked like he might be in his mid-twenties. He was obviously a foreigner, with his light skin, brown hair and blue eyes, but he was dressed like a sadhu. He carried a blanket and a water pot, a small bag with a few pieces of cloth and a couple of books. No one knew where he came from, but he spoke pure Bengali when he sat at the tea stall near the temple and asked for a cup of chai.

I was thirteen years old at the time, reading in the eighth grade, and he was the first white man I had ever seen. Some of my family were the Brahmin priests of the temple, and my father owned the shop that sold supplies and rented utensils at the cremation grounds. We thought we had seen a lot, having spent most of our lives in a Hindu temple atmosphere, and being so much a party to all of the rites of passage for all of the villagers in the vicinity. But this Sahib Sadhu[1] was fascinating to me, and I watched him from a distance, too intimidated to approach him.

Bakreshwar Village

After drinking a cup of tea from the little clay pots that we break after each service, he walked along the path past the bathing tank of the hot springs and the old banyan tree down to the river. I watched him bathe in the hottest part of the river, fed by the overflow from the hot springs.

He swam for a little while, and when he felt refreshed, he came out, took up his gamcha, a thin Indian towel, dried himself off and then changed his clothes. He took up his belongings and retraced his path back to the banyan tree, rolled out his asana,[2] and sat down under the tree in a yogic posture. He started to chant the most melodic Sanskrit I had ever heard, and then he closed his eyes and in a few minutes he was gone.

I had never seen anything like it before. His body was motionless, his breath appeared to have stopped and a most divine light emanated from his physical form. He was sitting right in

Swamiji in samadhi

front of me, and yet he seemed to have entered a realm that was light years away from the bustling village life surrounding his still form. A beatific smile graced his lips, but there was no sign of movement, no reaction to noise, no perspiration, not the slightest stir. He was in samadhi.

During those first weeks that he lived in the cremation grounds I merely watched him. He rose around three in the morning and sat in the hottest part of the hot springs. This water was so hot that sadhus[3] came all throughout the winter to sleep on the stones around the bathing tanks, yet few ventured to sit directly in the water. They tied up rice and dahl in a thin piece of cloth and threw the bundle into one of the tanks. It sank to the bottom as it started to cook. When the rice was boiled, it floated to the surface. Using a stick, they fished out the bundle, untied the cloth, added some masala[4] and other spices, and then sat down to eat.

Swamiji recited the entire *Chandi Path* in the morning while sitting in the hot springs. Then he performed yoga exercises. By dawn he returned to the banyan tree and organized his puja.[5] At first he performed his puja with whatever he could find: leaves, grass, grains of rice. Later, once we got to know him, the village children delighted in bringing him flowers for worship first thing every morning.

His worship lasted until 9:30 or 10:00. Then he took a short break for a half-hour or so before sitting down to sing the *Chandi* again. It was usually sometime after sunset that he rose from his seat. Then he took two bells, one in each hand, and rang them so loudly you could hear them resounding all the way across the village, while he sang the songs of arati.[6] Soon the whole village came to recognize the sounds of Swamiji's evening arati, and it became a topic of conversation around the whole village. Simply through his own constant, pure and unwavering private daily worship, this lone Sahib Sadhu had begun to change our lives.

Swamiji performing arati

Rishi Amritananda

We didn't know much about him, only what we saw, as well as a great collection of unconfirmed rumors that were passed around our village. He had traveled on foot throughout the Himalayas, and it was there that he had met his first Guru, the great Rishi Amritananda. When, as a young man, he first saw Amritananda,[7] the beloved sage was radiant with the light of his tapasya.[8] He later told me that he thought he was seeing Lord Shiva himself. On seeing this great Guru, he thought, "My God, what a privilege to study with such a man," and approached the sadhu. "I want to learn about sadhana. It would be a privilege for me if you will teach me," he said.

"Oh, you have come?" the holy man replied with great delight and love. "I have been waiting many years for you. Where were you all this time? Come, we must begin our work today. We have much to do. I am an old man and have little time to waste."

That evening the Guru invited his guest into his home. It was a small cave with a cozy fire, just big enough to accommodate two people. The whole night Amritananda spoke to his new pupil about the Sanatana Dharma, the eternal ideal of perfection. "My time is short, so you will have to learn quickly," Rishi Amritananda told him. "You will have to learn while enduring many hardships, with a minimum of food and sleep. You will have to learn the *Gita*, the *Chandi* and the *Ramayana*, and all the great literature of India. First we will study the *Vedas*." They continued in this way for a week, with little food or sleep.

It was only after spending seven days and nights in this man-

Caves where Swamiji did tapasya

ner that Rishi Amritananda felt he had a real disciple, an individual of unparalleled dedication and devotion. "Alexander the Great came to India to conquer the land, but you will conquer the soul," the guru told him. "He was doomed to failure, but you will not fail. You will be a true Guru. A day will come when you will spread your wisdom to both the Eastern and Western hemispheres, and you will have many followers on every continent. I give you my blessings."

Later that day Rishi Amritananda inquired, "If you want to stay and be a part of this country, you will need to travel with me to understand the life of a sadhu. Would you like to come with me on a spiritual pilgrimage?"

The young foreigner was ecstatic to have such an opportunity. "What shall I take with me?" inquired the eager student.

"Nothing. If you want to learn to rely on God, then take nothing with you. You only need to believe that everything you need will always be provided for you. Just take your faith and your longing to be with God."

The young man swallowed hard and thought deeply, wondering exactly what *nothing* meant. "Not even a credit card or traveler's checks?" he asked. "Nothing" replied his newfound Guru.

The youth was overcome with excitement, trepidation, fear and joy as the two prepared to set off on their journey. He knew that his life was about to change in extraordinary ways. He knew that his search of the past so many years was over. He had found his Guru. His life's work was about to begin.

Swamiji lost in worship

Kindling the Flame

Before embarking, the Guru said, "You will want to wear Indian clothes."

The foreign youth, who was wearing faded blue jeans and a T shirt, replied, "I don't know how to wear Indian clothes." So his new Guru showed him how to wrap a dhoti cloth around his waist. Rishi Amritananda taught the young man many things great and small. Their first evening in the forest, the youth sat down in a clearing and started asking his teacher some of the many questions he had carried with him for years while on his search for true wisdom. "Wait," answered Amritananda. "All the philosophy in the world will not keep you warm at night. First, you must learn to build a fire."

"What does that have to do with enlightenment?" asked the youth. "I come from a country where that kind of knowledge is no longer necessary. We merely set the thermostat to the desired temperature, and the heating or air-conditioning automatically adjusts the environment accordingly."

"Because you have lived in such an artificial environment, your mind has moved away from its most natural state. You have sacrificed your peace for comfort. They are diametrically opposed," replied the Guru. "The amount of comfort that an individual pursues is equal to the amount of peace that flees from him. As much as one may try to satisfy the body, that much is the dissatisfaction of the mind. In your movement back to the most natural state of peaceful mind, which is the birthright of every human being, you must sacrifice your comforts as well as your confusions, which are born from conflicting attachments. Now, learn how to make a fire."

Rishi Amritananda showed the young man how to choose and mix gathered pieces of wood such that he could quickly get a good fire going with maximum heating potential. He taught him to look for kindling that was naturally soaked with pine pitch so that he could start a fire even with wet wood. He taught his new student how to make friends with the fire and how to treat it with respect, allowing just enough oxygen to get in to allow it to burn, but not so much that it burned out quickly and he froze half the night.

Swamiji lighting the homa fire

Satyananda Is Born

The young foreigner knew absolutely nothing about Indian culture, let alone living in the forest, and his Guru spent hours every day teaching the eager disciple about the strange, rich, vast culture and history of this ancient land of India. They passed many days together in this manner.

He taught him how to take food: "You must use your hands to eat. Your hands are God's spoon," he told him.

He taught him how to sit in meditation: "Every movement of the body is a reflection of the movement of the mind. In order to hold your mind still, you must make your physical body sit still."

He taught him how to chant Sanskrit mantras, "*Man trayate iti mantra*, that which takes away your mind. *San* means 'all together' and *kri* means 'to do.' Our language of communication is literally, 'What we do together.' The *mantras* that we do together take us out of our minds and into the realms of intuitive experience."

Despite enduring these great hardships, the young man never gave up. He walked continuously with his Guru and learned about the Sanskrit language, the *Vedas* and the *Upanishads*.

After six months of walking together through forest and field, town and village, on the flat river bottom and over high mountain passes, they came upon a cave where his Guru thought they should rest for awhile. It was then that his next phase of learning began. "We will sit here for some time," said Rishi Amritananda. "Then we will take a vow not to sit under any constructed roof for the next three years."

With those words they began the study of the revered *Rig*

Veda and the disciple started to learn the method of worship called *yagya*, involving an intricately beautiful fire ceremony. Some of their yagyas lasted for five days, some for seven, some for twenty-one, one hundred and eight, and even one thousand days. (In fact, on four occasions Swamiji has performed the *Sahasra Chandi Yagya*. Each one of these yagyas lasted one thousand days — three full years each – and involved continuous practice of his spiritual disciplines without moving from the sacrificial fire for even a single day. In total, Swamiji has thus far spent twelve years of his life performing the famous *Sahasra Chandi Yagya*, a discipline described in the *Puranas* but rarely performed in modern times.)

The student devoted six years to learning all that he could about the fire ceremony, *homa* and *yagya*.[9] After Swamiji mastered the fire ceremonies, he turned to learning the *Chandi Path* and then to the *Devi Bhagavatam* and *Bhagavat Gita*, and studied the other *Vedas*, *Puranas* and *Itihas* or Histories of India. He mastered them all in their entirety and then shared his knowledge of the Vedic scriptures as a brilliant and engaging storyteller.

Pleased with his disciple's accomplishments, Rishi Amritananda named him *Satyananda*, the Bliss of Truth. In giving him his new name, Amritananda told him: "From now on you can forget about your past life, your past names, your past memories. You are now the Bliss of Truth. You belong to the world. You will help many people find peace. The entire world will see your example, and will want to laugh and sing with you. But first you must perform tapasya, purifying austerities. You must learn and practice how to sit, how to chant, how to breathe. Only then will you be able to recognize true divinity."

Bakreswar

It was 1970 that Rishi Amritananda and his disciple came to Bakreswar. My life changed that year because the man who was to become my Swamiji soon became an important part of it. Satyananda and his Guru stayed in a little hut near the cremation grounds. "I will meditate here in honor of the Sadhu Bakra," said Amritananda. Legend has it that Sadhu Bakra meditated for sixty thousand years in that place. It is said that when he was still in his mother's womb, he heard his father chanting the *Vedas*. To his father's utter dismay, he heard his unborn child say, "You are making many mistakes. Your ego is still controlling you." His father, furious at his unborn child for speaking to him in such a manner, cursed his son, pronouncing: "You will be born deformed!" When the child was born, all his fingers were grossly bent. "What curse have you placed on your own son?" cried his horrified mother. The now pacified husband reassured his wife that if the boy meditated for a thousand years, he would please Shiva and the curse would be lifted. "The boy will become a great sadhu," he said.

And his father was right. After performing austerities for a thousand years, Shiva was pleased and blessed Sadhu Bakra. By that time the sadhu's hair had grown incredibly long.[10] He spread it out in seven different directions, and from each of these seven points hot water sprang from underground. Bakranath[11] is still the source of this hot water.

When Satyananda reached Bakreswar, he bathed in the sacred hot waters and began his meditation. He rose before dawn, bathed and meditated. Afterwards, he visited the local villagers, both the destitute and the rich, and learned about the local customs and Indian culture. After performing his daily spiritual practices, Satyananda spent hours discussing the Vedic scriptures and other teachings with his beloved Guru, often continuing late into the night. This was the beginning of Satyananda's sojourn in Bakreswar.

When I first saw Satyananda perform a yagya, his poise and blissful aura struck me. I had never seen a sadhu like this before. I did not speak any English at the time, so I just observed him quietly. I was just a boy of thirteen. Yet I kept coming back to see him. I couldn't resist. Every time I saw him, I was very tempted to approach and speak to him, but I couldn't muster up the courage to do so. Finally one full week later after I first laid eyes on him, I finally spoke to him. I told Satyananda that I wanted to see him perform puja and meditate. He smiled and replied, "Come any day. If you come in the morning, you will see my daily program. Some days I do puja, other days I do homa, and I recite the *Chandi*." So I gratefully accepted his kind invitation. That was the beginning of my spiritual adventure.

The Test at the Fire

One day Rishi Amritananda invited all the villagers, educated and illiterate, affluent and destitute alike, to witness the performance of a yagya. The local priests came as well. The fire was to be lit in the traditional manner, by simply rubbing two sticks of wood together. These sticks are called *Arani* and *Matandanda*. All who were present were invited to try to light the fire. The priests laughed and said, "Only a Brahmin can light the fire by the Vedic method." Everyone who tried failed to light the fire. Then the Guru called upon Satyananda. Pensively, doubtfully, Satyananda began the task. With trembling hands he began to rub the sticks together. His face turned red with the effort, his hands became blistered, and still Satyananda continued rubbing, all the time chanting sacred mantras for the yagya. Finally, after persisting for two full hours, Satyananda lit the yagya fire. Having witnessed his one-pointed focus on the task, and his unstoppable will to succeed in the assignment his beloved Guru had given him, the crowd that had assembled were overjoyed.

As soon as the embers came to life, the people all around him started shouting, "Swami Satyananda ki jai!"[12] The Brahmins in attendance then acknowledged that Satyananda was their peer, and his Guru was very proud of his worthy disciple. Once the much anticipated fire had been lit, Rishi Amritananda and the other priests started the homa, which continued all night long, not ending until eight o'clock the following morning. This was one of the many milestones achieved in Satyananda's remarkable life.

Overcoming Prejudice

My friends, like most of the villagers, were skeptical of the mysterious sahib. Some were even contemptuous. One old priest, Ashok Mukhapadhyay, however, said that Satyananda was not a fraud, but his words went unheeded. Satyananda was jeered at and mocked by many of the townspeople, especially the haughty Brahmin priests. "Go back to your own country, you foreigner! You will never learn our culture. It will take you a thousand years to do so. People will come to us when they want something. Why should they go to you?" Satyananda paid them no attention and kept chanting, meditating and studying, as his Guru had instructed him.

Within a few months, though, even these egotistical priests began to realize that the older priest who had offered respect to Satyananda was right. This man was no joke. Satyananda proved his worth to them in many ways, and they finally began to treat him with respect and started being more hospitable to him. Once he gained their respect, Satyananda started to share some of his remarkable stories and gems of wisdom with the villagers.

I became his friend, his student, his assistant. I had the honor of bringing him food and being with him constantly. I ate with him and slept on the ground near him. Every day after school I visited Satyananda. I was lucky in that my parents were so supportive. They supplied us with food and allowed me to spend so much of my time in the company of this great man.

I passed many happy days with Satyananda under a mango tree by the bank of the river. He taught me English and Sanskrit and many subjects. Within a short period of time, all the villagers had grown to love, admire and respect Satyananda. He and Guru Amritananda stayed in Bakreswar for many years. They studied, meditated, cooked, gardened and spent time with the local villagers.

Shiva Baba ki jai!

The Rainmaker

For some reason the gods became angry with the village of Bakreswar. It was 1972 and it had not rained properly for ten years. Livestock died of hunger and thirst, and the crops refused to grow. The miserable farmers toiled fruitlessly on arid land, parched from the relentless sun. The village priests performed their pujas in vain, beseeching the gods to bring them rain, but their prayers went unheeded. As a last resort, some of the farmers decided to approach the mysterious foreign sadhu and ask for his help. "We are in a terrible condition. Please perform a yagya to appease the wrathful gods and bring us rain. We will gladly make any provisions you require." Swamiji only replied, "I need nothing but your pure love."

It was the last week in September when Satyananda began his fire ceremony to Indra, the God of Rain. On the first day of the Indra yagya, Satyananda prayed to all the heavenly deities. The entire village was present. The egotistical priests looked on contemptuously and sniggered. "Look at the audacity of this insolent foreigner. He thinks he can succeed where even we, the priests of this village, have failed."

For four days Swamiji tirelessly continued his yagya rites from early morning until late at night. When the fifth day had passed, the villagers lost hope and felt that Satyananda too would not succeed.

Then on the sixth day, the skies darkened in the morning and it started drizzling by afternoon. By nightfall, there was a torrential downpour, which continued throughout the entire day and night of the seventh day. By the eighth day the entire village, once dying for its dearth of water, was inundated. Many homes had been washed away and destruction was everywhere. People were trapped in what remained of their homes because of the magnitude of the flooding. Many people spent the entire night on their rooftops in order to escape the raging flood waters. The entire district was declared a national disaster area.

By dusk of the eighth day, the waters began to subside. The place where Satyananda had been performing the yagya was completely submerged in water. No one had dared to venture to the spot and risk dying in the rush of water. But as the skies calmed and the flooding subsided, our villagers began whispering amongst themselves. "We cannot see Satyananda anywhere. What happened to Satyananda? He must have perished in the floods. He did not even have a real home in this village. We must find his body if possible."

On the morning of the ninth day, some of the villagers took a boat and went to the spot where they had last seen Satyananda. I was among them. We searched all over for his body, but he was nowhere to be found. Suddenly someone exclaimed, "I can hear the sound of chanting from up in that big tree over there!" We all looked up and, to our utter amazement, there was Satyananda sitting on a branch in that tree, still chanting his *Chandi Path*. He was offering leaves from the tree as his puja.

On seeing us, Satyananda, soaking wet and shaking with cold, came down from the tree and blessed those present, "I know you have all suffered. Indra is now pleased, and you will all benefit from these rains." The shame-faced priests who had not believed in Swamiji, offered him dry clothing and sweets. Satyananda blessed them and asked them to pray with greater sincerity. Only then would they succeed in their spiritual quest.

The villagers now had all the evidence they needed to know that they were in the presence of a genuine Rishi. Satyananda became the adopted son of our village. He was always welcome in every home. People looked forward to the honor of hosting him. Yet he always resided in the cremation grounds.

Swamiji singing in the village

Feeding All Who Cometh

It was in 1974 in Bakreswar that Satyananda performed a small, fifteen-day yagya in a temple located under a banyan tree. The tree was named *Akshaybatabriksha*, which literally means "the indestructible banyan tree." The area around the temple and tree was home to many poisonous snakes, especially the deadly cobras.

We had all been visiting Satyananda regularly for the first fourteen days of the fire ceremony, but none of us spent the night in the temple with him. On the fifteenth day Swamiji sent for me, a few of my friends and some other devotees. He wanted us to make rice pudding. We did as he requested and made enough for about one hundred people. Once it was prepared, we put the sweet rice pudding in a pot with a ladle and covered it with a piece of cloth. We all spent the night at the temple, watching the yagya with Satyananda, because he instructed us not to leave the temple premises under any circumstances. The yagya was to end the following morning.

At the end of the ceremony the next morning, Satyananda called us over to the window, which afforded us a clear view of the banyan tree. "Look closely under that tree," he said placidly. What we saw made our blood run cold. There, out in the darkness, were three large cobras, standing deathly still with their hoods raised. "That is why I instructed you not to go outside. These are not ordinary snakes. They are heavenly visitors who have come to observe this yagya. Had you disturbed them, you might have experienced difficulties," Satyananda said, as he shut the window. "I will recite mantras for these three snakes so they can return to their own home." He sat in deep meditation for a few minutes, blessed our amazed band of witnesses and bade us to wait patiently for a little while. When Satyananda let us know that it was alright, we all eagerly looked under the banyan tree, but we could not find any trace of our strange, celestial guests.

The yagya had come to a close. Satyananda invited the villagers and priests to his temple and instructed us to serve the rice pudding we had prepared the previous night. It seemed obvious, from the number of guests who arrived at the temple, that there would not be enough to feed everyone. We shared our concern with Satyananda. "Keep the cloth covering on the pot and just serve the rice pudding," he assured us. "God is happy with pure devotion and pure love." With great hesitation we began to serve the guests.

After we had fed one hundred people, we were sure we would run out, but the pot was still full. After two hundred people had eaten, we thought, "This is impossible. We didn't make enough rice pudding to feed two hundred people," but as long as the people kept coming, the pot was never empty. Finally, when the night was over, to our great astonishment, we discovered we had served five hundred people equally generous portions of rice pudding and still had plenty left over in the pot! Like this pot of pudding, our hearts never felt a shortage of God's blessings around Satyananda.

Swami

After spending twelve years with his Guru, Satyananda was ready to become a Swami. He performed a yagya for seven days and fed a thousand people with kicheri he made himself, combining rice, dahl and vegetables with spices and condiments. At dusk he bathed in the river. Then his Guru sat with him at the sacred fire, and the two worshipped at the yagya together. They chanted mantras from the *Mahanirvana Tantra, Rig Veda* and *Chandi Path*. The homa continued late into the night.

Then the Guru offered him some water and sweets, and with blessings said, "From this day you are Swami Satyananda Saraswati. *Swa* means one's own. *Ami* means I am. *Swami* means, 'I am my own.' This means you are your own master, qualified to teach. There are two initiations that every Swami must take. The first is from your teacher, which I am giving to you now. Your next initiation will be given to you by your disciples. It is one thing for me to say that you are qualified to teach. It is another thing all together for your disciples to say that you have something that they want to learn."

It was an important step for Swamiji. Even having received the authority from above to teach in his Master's lineage, Swamiji still couldn't imagine that he would actually become a teacher. He thought of himself as an eternal student, a disciple, and wanted nothing more than to remain in study and continual practice. Now his Guru was saying that he wouldn't remain a disciple for long. He was a Swami. This had an impact on Swamiji. He couldn't help but feel a greater sense of commitment to his spiritual discipline. Now it was no longer just his practice. It was his life.

Amritananda's Maha Samadhi

Rishi Amritananda passed away in 1976, after completing a thousand day yagya. He sat in his asana before a group of disciples who had gathered near to him. Swamiji was there too. Before he left his body, Guruji told me that Swamiji was now a true Master. "Sushil," he said, "Swamiji will fulfill my asana. He will be a Master of all spiritual knowledge and will transmit that knowledge to others. Stay with him if possible. You will be happy. He will travel all over the world and spread goodness. He will take over my karma and do his duty. He will do this work for fifty or sixty years."

"He will travel the world and perform yagyas for peace. He will give light and wisdom, and many people will come to him. At an old age his work will be finished, and only then he will leave his earthly body. These are my final words to you."

Rishi Amritananda gave his final blessings, and while still sitting in his yogic posture, he left his body. Swamiji performed the last rites and cremation himself. He enkindled the yagya fire beneath his Guru's body and then recited the entire *Chandi*, offering oblations to its flames. There was never greater respect shown by any disciple to the passing of his Master.

Swamiji was now on his own. This was the beginning of another phase in his memorable journey.

Sadhana

As long as Swamiji lived in Bakreswar, his daily habit was to sit in the hot springs under a fountain shaped like an elephant's mouth. The water was so hot that most people could only splash about or sit in it for a little while. It was a popular spot for tourists from Calcutta to test their endurance and show off to their friends that they could splash the hot water from the elephant's mouth on their bodies. Most people who went there made lots of noise.

Swamiji used to sit under the fountain for three hours every morning and recite the entire *Chandi Path* in the hottest water. Then he would get up and perform hatha yoga exercises on the deck, again wash in the hot spring, and then visit all the temples in Bakreswar and offer puja. His sadhana in Bakreswar continued in this way all year long. He endured all seasons of weather and continued ceaselessly in the rhythm of his spiritual discipline.

In the same manner, I noticed that while living in Rishikesh, he used to immerse himself daily in the cold waters of the Ganga[13] and recite the *Chandi Path* for three hours. In fact, one winter morning it was so cold that by the time he finished his recitation, he couldn't get any feeling back into his limbs. Some sadhus saw his difficulty and raced into the freezing waters to rescue him and assist him coming out of the river.

For the most part, in all that I have observed, Swamiji was undaunted by both hot and cold. He was always the same and was consistent in his sadhana.

One night, when Swamiji was returning from the cremation grounds, he became sick with a high fever and vomiting. Both Pachu, a devotee from our village, and I were with him at the time. We told Swamiji that we would go to the nearest doctor in the next village. Swamiji replied, "Don't go. I'll be OK."

Pachu and I went to the village doctor's house anyway. It was two in the morning. The doctor was surprised when we woke him at such an hour. "Swamiji?" he inquired. "He is a great sadhu. He will cure himself with his meditation. Did he really send you for medicine, or did you come of your own accord?" Worried about our beloved Swamiji, we persisted and again requested, "Please give us some medicine. He seems very sick." So the doctor acquiesced and gave us medicine for Swamiji.

When we returned an hour later, we saw Swamiji sitting contentedly on his meditation seat. He opened his eyes and was happy to see us. "Please make some food," he requested. We did and Swamiji happily ate his dinner.

This is the character of meditation. Adepts in higher states of meditation have gained mastery over their bodies and can heal themselves with the power of their sadhana. Such saintly beings do these kinds of things by manifesting and working with divine energies.

While listening to this story, Shree Maa commented: "He was in a high state. He could take everything from this world, and he could dissolve."

Swami in samadhi naked on the snow

Curing Pachu's Daughter

Pachu's daughter was very sick. She could not eat or sleep. There was a bad smell coming from her body. Everyone said she would die. Pachu's wife came to Swamiji and said, "All the doctors have done what they can, but they cannot help her. They have all given up hope. Can you help?"

Swamiji replied, "I will give you another doctor. I will send your daughter to Maa Shakti, the Divine Mother Healer. If Maa says your daughter will die, she will die. If Maa says she will live, then she will live." Swamiji performed a yagya and put ashes from the yagya first on Pachu's daughter's head and feet, then all over her body, while chanting healing mantras. She was immediately soothed.

Swamiji then instructed, "I will come here every day for nine days and apply these ashes to the child's body. She will be OK. Now stop all your worrying and channel all your energy into prayer. Prayer is much more effective than worrying. What the Divine wills, will be. We can influence the Divine will with prayer much more than with worry."

The child's Mother cried out, "But Swamiji, she is dying." Swami reassured her, once again that her daughter would get better, and then left. And Pachu's daughter did get better and was completely cured.

When I saw her a few years later, she was so beautiful. Now she has a daughter and son of her own.

Curing Hem, a Leper

Kandu had a son whose name was Hem. Kandu was a farmer, a good man and a devotee of Swamiji. He was a simple and humble man, who helped his neighbors as much as he could. At one point in time, he started visiting a man who was pretending to be a Swami. This fake Swami had a dog and a fox. The fake Swami told Kandu to feed the fox every day. When our Swamiji found out about this, he told Kandu not to touch the fox, but Kandu didn't listen. One day the fox bit Kandu and he fell down, and then became bedridden with fever. He became mad and then died.

Then, even though Swamiji had told him not to go, Kandu's son Hem also started going to this fake Swami. Hem became afflicted with leprosy. For a few months he stopped visiting Swamiji. So one day Swamiji asked us why Hem wasn't coming any more. We told him that Hem had leprosy, which made him untouchable, so he had become separated from society. No one would even eat the fruits and vegetables produced from his land.

When Swamiji learned of Hem's disease, he immediately went to his house to visit him. Swamiji went inside the house and saw Hem lying down in his bed. Swamiji picked Hem up in his arms and hugged him and then began to sing and dance. Everyone was astounded. "He is suffering from God's disease, devarog,"[14] they said.

But Swamiji held onto Hem's hands and said, "I told you not to go there. Now your fingers have leprosy." Then Swamiji chanted, wrapped Hem's hands in leaves and instructed Hem's relatives to continue this treatment. Every day Hem's hands were wrapped in leaves, and his leprosy went away.

Swamiji then explained his actions to us: "Untouchability is the disease. We should hate the disease, but not the people who are diseased. All human beings are our family."

Leprosy is called devarog, the disease of the Gods

Inspiring Ideal Marriage

There was a priest in our temple who was always quarreling with his wife. Every day he came to the temple in such a grumpy mood, and he always complained about his wife. One day Swamiji was walking near the house of his family and the priest invited him inside for a cup of tea. The priest asked him, "Why don't you come to study Sanskrit with the priests inside the temple?"

Swamiji replied, "I think the people who practice Sanskrit should be sharing joy and inspiration in their communications, and they should desire to live in the harmony of their spiritual commitment. In fact, everything I have learned about the Sanskrit vows of marriage solemnize the promise to be a constant reminder to your partner of his or her own divinity. That is, the only reason we get married according to dharma is to be the constant inspiration for our partner's divine expression. That's what the mantras of the marriage ceremony say."

On hearing this, the priest bowed down to Swamiji and never complained about his wife again. Even the neighbors have told me that they never heard them argue after Swamiji's visit to their house.

Bringing Calm to the Departed

In the early 1970s the Naxalite Movement[15] had spread throughout northeast India. Many men lost their lives due to the political unrest borne of that movement. While abiding in a region of India overtaken by such strife, one day Swamiji came upon a skeleton. Only the bones remained. During the night he often saw a vision of this man hanging from a tree with no blood or skin. This recurred time and again, and he came to realize that this man had died under violent circumstances in an inappropriate way.

After seeing this repeatedly, Swamiji came to understand that this man's soul had become a ghost. So he set out to locate the man's surviving relatives. Once he found them, he learned that the family had been suffering from many problems since the death of this man. So he told them of his visions and instructed them to go to Gaya and offer a memorial ceremony for the departed, and to offer flowers to the feet of Lord Visnu.

Gaya is the most important center for honoring the departed, and the presiding deity is Lord Vishnu. Even Rama and Lakshman went to Gaya to offer prayers for the peace of their father's soul. Once the family performed the ceremony for their departed relative as instructed by Swamiji, all of their family's problems disappeared. And this was how the ghost became free.

The Snake Charmer

Swamiji used to bathe in the hot springs in our village early every morning. Then he would chant the *Chandi* and meditate while sitting in the hot water. One morning, while lying under the hot water spout, a large cobra came and sat on his chest. Swamiji looked at the cobra and the cobra coiled, with his hood flared out, and looked directly into Swamiji's eyes, perched only a few inches away from his face. The two were locked in a staring competition, and Swamiji did not blink even once.

I learned of Swami's predicament when Pachu came running into the courtyard of my house, shouting, "Sushil Babu, Sushil Babu! Certainly Swamiji is going to die today!" I woke up with a start and ran out into the courtyard. "What are you talking about?" I inquired.

Pachu was out of breath, but managed to reply, "A cobra is sitting on Swamiji's chest, about to strike him dead. They are in the hot springs."

I grabbed a shawl and pulled it around me as I ran out the door. When I got to the hot springs it was almost dawn, and half the village was standing on the far side of the pool looking at Swamiji, who was still staring at the cobra. "Certainly the Sahib Sadhu is going to die today," they said in a matter of fact tone.

I was terrified and really worried about Swamiji's safety. I even started fretting over the potential loss of my beloved Guru. It had been close to three hours that Swamiji and the snake were locked in *tratak*, the practice of staring deeply into one another's eyes, and everyone was awaiting the impending strike, which would bring inevitable doom. Swamiji was softly repeating the

mantra, *Om Namah Shivaya*, again and again to appease the cobra, because Shiva is the God of the snakes, but the cobra just
kept staring into his eyes.

No one could think of anything we could do to save him. We
were afraid to try to frighten the snake, for fear that he would
strike, and no other good options came to mind. Suddenly, the
cobra closed his hood, put his head down and slithered away
through the hot water. Swamiji was saved! He had outstared the
cobra, and by surrendering to the will of Shiva through chanting
his mantra, he had averted disaster. Swamiji's sadhana had such
power that he knew that he was being tested, and he stood up to
the challenge. When face to face with imminent death, his thoughts
became absorbed in God, and that brought him the stillness that
saved him from danger. Everyone let out a shout of triumph, and
after helping him out of the hot water, they all bowed down to
him and touched his feet.

Clothed in Space

One of Swamiji's disciples, Pachu, worked in the cremation grounds. Pachu's job was to cremate the dead bodies. As part of his job, he collected the oil emitted from the nostrils of the burning corpses and collected the ashes of the burned corpses. Whenever he had free time from his duties, Pachu went to Swamiji and gave him an oil massage with the oil he had collected from the cremations. So when Swamiji had pain in his joints, he sent for Pachu.

One year during the winter time, Swamiji was *digambar*, literally "clothed in space." His only clothing was a loin cloth and ashes. That is known as the *sadhana of digambar*. Many men came from the neighboring villages to see Swamiji. He looked like Lord Shiva himself, sitting in meditation. Having a sadhu perform such a great tapasya in one's village is considered to be a great blessing. So it was in this way that Swamiji chose to bless the people of that area and thus make them happy.

By performing this practice Swamiji demonstrated that this body we spend our entire lives worrying over is impermanent, and only the invincible atma, or eternal soul, is real. The individual "ego I" is only a bundle of attachments to the transient illusions of life. By rubbing the oil and ashes from the cremated bodies onto his own body, he showed that the truly enlightened spirit is not attached to the physical body. He was free from all attachments. He wanted nothing but to serve humankind and sing to God. As I look at and reflect on his present actions and work, I believe he still wants the same things.

Defending the Untouchables

One day the Police Station Master came to see Swamiji and was praising him and telling him what a great man he was. Pachu came over to sit with them. The policeman asked Pachu his name. Pachu replied, "Pachu Dom." The policeman immediately became upset and said to Pachu, "*Dom* means that you work in the cremation grounds. You are untouchable. What are you doing defiling Swamiji's ashram? I refuse to talk to you!"

Swamiji became angry and exclaimed loudly to the policeman, "Pachu is our brother! All the men who work in the cremation grounds provide a pure service and earn an honest livelihood. When we die they prepare our bodies to be received in heaven. Why are they untouchable? If he takes a bath after coming from his work, then he is clean! How is it that you praise the Guru and despise the disciples? I have no need for such praise!"

The "Drunken" Sadhu

At times Swamiji stayed in the little hut next to the cremation grounds and meditated after midnight next to the funeral pyres. One day, when coming back from the cremation grounds, a group of visitors from Calcutta started joking that this white man, even though he was white, could not walk steadily. They said that he was staggering like a drunk. Then they began shouting that this foreigner had come to destroy our religion, and said he would teach our children to drink and take intoxicants. While carrying on in this way, they surged toward Swamiji screaming, "Beat that man!"

Swamiji just continued quietly on his way. Pachu was walking beside him. He loved Swamiji so very much. On hearing the crowd, Pachu called to me to come at once. I came immediately with some of my friends. "What are you doing causing such commotion in our village?" we demanded of the visitors from Calcutta. "You are the ones destroying our religion!"

Pachu picked up a big stick and threatened, "I will beat them!" Swamiji put up his hand and stopped us all from going any further. "Loving all beings is my religion. Please don't fight over whether or not I am drunk. When a dog bites someone, will you go and bite the dog back? The love of human beings is the love of God. The truth is I am drunk with the love of God, not with the consumption of alcohol."

Once they heard these divine teachings from Swamiji, the visitors from Calcutta bowed down and touched his feet. "We were going to beat you, but please forgive us, Swamiji. Now, we know that you are a great soul who has come to bless us."

Appeasing the Ghosts

One day Swamiji invited us to go to Tarapith to perform a yagya, the sacred fire ceremony. It was Amavasya, the night of the new moon. I went with Swamiji, accompanied by a number of friends. We reached Tarapith at ten in the morning and collected all the wood, ghee, rice and flowers required for the ceremony. We selected a place in the cremation grounds for our worship, and Swamiji built the yagya vedi.[16] He drew the yantra, or sacred symbol, upon which the fire would sit, and we started our homa at seven thirty in the evening.

Swamiji told us that the fire would burn until the following morning. He told us that the Goddess Tara would be happy with our efforts, and that several of the ghosts would be freed from the cremation grounds when the yagya was completed.

Swamiji made a big circle and invited all twenty or so of us to sit inside the circle. He instructed that no one should leave the circle while the fire was burning. It was very strange to us, but we didn't worry about it. We noticed that there a goat and her kid standing outside the circle, but there were always plenty of goats around in such villages, so we didn't pay them much attention. At about three in the morning the yagya was completed, and Swamiji told us, "Eat your food now and then go to sleep here. But don't go outside the circle."

As we were going to sleep, we noticed that the goat and her kid were still standing in the same place, but we still did not pay much attention to them.

In the morning after we awoke and got up, Swamiji asked us how we felt about the yagya. We told him that we felt it had gone well.

"Did you see anything special?" he asked us. "Did you not see a goat and her kid?"

"Yes," we replied. "We remember seeing a goat standing over there outside the circle." The goat was still standing in the same place.

"Why was the goat standing there, and why was I telling you not to go outside the circle?" Swamiji asked.

We told him we did not know.

He explained, "The goat was a lady who in her past life had committed suicide and had killed her small child, and they had become ghosts of goats. If you had gone outside the circle, she could have harmed you. I took the ashes from the yagya and blessed their bodies, and by wearing those ashes all over their bodies, these goats were freed, liberated from that karma. It was for that purpose that we came here for this yagya.

"I told her that committing suicide is a sin. How can you destroy this body that is a temple of God? Everyone should take care of the body. It is because of the body that we can do puja and worship god."

This is how Swamiji taught us.

Meeting Bamakshepa

Bamakshepa was a legend in northeastern India. He was one hundred and eighty years old and he was invisible. Bamakshepa was a devotee of the Divine Mother and remained naked most of the time. He always had a black dog with him. Before he disappeared, he said that only the great ones would be able to see him. Then he was nowhere to be found.

One morning Swamiji decided he wanted to meet Bamakshepa. So Swamiji, a few other devotees and I went to the forest near Tarapith where Bamakshepa was last known to be reportedly living. Swamiji took off all of his clothes and began to walk into the forest. Suddenly, out of nowhere, a black dog appeared. Swamiji said to us, "You should stay here," and he turned and followed the black dog into the forest. Then they both disappeared. No Swami, no dog.

After about twelve hours, we suddenly saw the dog appear and then Swamiji. Then the dog went back into the forest. Swamiji was laughing and telling us, "It was so beautiful! He said that he had been waiting for years for me. He blessed me and taught me many things. I am extremely happy and want to dance!" He was in an ecstatic superconscious state and danced for an hour fully naked. Then he sat down and slept.

We took him back to the ashram and took care of him and he gradually came back to his natural state of consciousness.

Examination Gifts

It was time to take the final examinations for my master's degree. Swamiji was living in Bakreswar during this period, and I had come to know him very well by then. One day I confessed nervously to him, "I am not prepared for these exams."

"Put your mind at rest and just take the examinations, Sushil," Swamiji advised me. I took his blessings, bid my parents farewell and left Bakreswar for Burdwan, where I was assigned to take my examinations.

I arrived at my lodgings, the Chittaranjan Hostel, and found all my friends diligently studying. To my consternation, I found that I had forgotten everything I knew about my subject. It was two nights before the examinations were to begin and I was unable to write a single word, let alone string together sentences. So I decided not to take the examinations and went to bed.

To this very day I cannot explain what happened to me that night. Swamiji appeared to me in a dream and said, "It will be a mistake not to take the exams. I will give you a mantra to help you." And he whispered a mantra in my ear during my dream.

When I woke up the next morning, my mind was a complete blank. I could not decide what my next course of action should be. All I could think of was the mantra I had received the previous night during my sleep. I was still thinking about what I should do when I got news that Swamiji had arrived at the hostel where I was staying. I was surprised and thrilled to see him. All one hundred students living there were astonished to see this foreign sage. After being introduced to everyone in attendance and offering his blessings to the crowd that gathered around him,

Swamiji ate dinner with all of us delighted students in the hostel's dining hall.

At around eleven o'clock that night, Swamiji told us he was leaving the hostel. Our curiosity was piqued. "But where are you going at this late hour?" we asked him. His only reply was "Burdwan 108 Shiva Mandir." We all looked at each other apprehensively. It was common knowledge that this was a temple that was located in an unsafe area. It was built two centuries ago by the Maharaja of Burdwan, King Krishnachandra.

"There is nothing to fear," Swamiji assured us. "I have stayed in that temple many times before." So after blessing us again, he departed.

The following day was the first day of my master's examinations. To my great surprise, I did wonderfully! In the evening, after the exam period, Swamiji came to the hostel from the temple where he was staying and blessed all of us students. He continued to come every night until our examinations were over.

With Swamiji on our side, it was not so surprising that we all did very well on our respective exams. On the last day Swamiji generously brought us Burdwan's famous Sitabhog sweets. As he handed them out, he blessed the enchanted group: "May God's

love and blessings be with you all."

And I was certain that I had been enchanted when I learned that I had passed all of my examinations!

The Whole World Is Our Family

One fall morning after having performed a nine-day Durga Puja ceremony at Virananda's Ashram, Swamiji returned to Bakreswar, where he resided for a few days. One day he turned to me and suggested, "Why don't you stay with me? We can travel together. You will have no difficulty finding food and lodging if you come with me."

I felt my mind crying out to him, and went home and told my parents about the invitation. They immediately shared in my excitement. "Go and tour India with Swamiji, son," they instructed me. "It will be an unforgettable adventure."

I was so excited. I would have the opportunity to be in Swamiji's company constantly and have him all to myself! I would fill my eyes with his radiant presence and weep many tears of ineffable joy and bliss. I cannot even begin to fully describe the happiness I felt at this time. I had endured much pain and suffering in my short life up to that time. Now, ever since having become a serious full-time disciple of Swamiji, I have been able to experience and appreciate happiness whenever it comes my way.

The following morning Swamiji and I left Bakreswar and got on a train at Dubrajpur. While traveling together on the train, Swamiji told me that our relationship had started many lifetimes before. "Today you are setting out to travel with me throughout India," he said. "Someday you will find yourself traveling with me around the world. Remember: *Vasudeva Kutumbakam*. The whole world is our family. We will travel the world like a dancing Shiva, holding and joining the hands of many people."

I listened to his words with rapt attention. Suddenly I saw

that Swamiji was in deep meditation. He did not wake from it even when we reached the train station in Deoghar, which is very famous for its Shiva Temple. In his meditation Swamiji looked like Lord Shiva himself. Countless people thronged about in the train station and touched his feet.

Our arrival at Deogarh was on an auspicious occasion: it was the day of Kojagiri Lakshmi Puja.[17] Swamiji and I walked until we reached Balananda Brahmachari Ashram, a distance of five or six kilometers. There we found Mohananda Brahmachari[18] performing his puja; his whole body was covered with gold jewelry. He had a huge pradeep,[19] with several layers of wicks dipped in ghee that were burning with great illumination, and he was doing an arati that lasted for an hour. During the arati, Swamiji, looking like a god himself, was deeply absorbed in meditation. The place was teeming with people, all waiting to partake of Lakshmi's prasad.[20] All of a sudden, Mohananda came up to Swamiji and embraced him, saying in a loud voice, "Lord Narayana himself has arrived on the day of Lakshmi's Puja!"

Swamiji embraced him back and both started discussing idealistic philosophy with great energy. Mohananda took us back into the ashram and wanted to make arrangements for us to eat elsewhere. Swamiji refused. He wanted to eat in the temple with the poor and destitute they were feeding, so he sat down and ate prasad with them. After we finished eating, Swamiji said, "We will stay in the Shiva Temple." That night we went to a small Shiva Temple and Swamiji began meditating. Like a child I lay my head on his knee and fell asleep. My new life had begun.

After our morning bath, we went to the Vaidyanath Shiva Temple. At the entrance we found a line of at least a thousand people. I never imagined we would ever get the darshan[21] of Vaidyanath Shiva. Suddenly a man whom I surmised to be a priest came over to Swamiji and took us inside the temple. We did not even have to stand in line. Once we were inside, we turned around to thank him, and he had disappeared. It was as though Vaidyanath Shiva himself had come to escort us inside his temple. After completing our Shiva Puja, we went back outside. On seeing him, countless people started worshipping Swamiji as the embodiment of Lord Shiva. They placed flowers on his feet and asked for his blessings. With his fair skin and white clothing, Swamiji did look like an incarnation of Shiva.

Eventually the crowds dispersed and we found a small clearing in the nearby forest, where Swamiji meditated for about four hours. He then asked me to bring him some prasad. After eating, we started walking towards the Deoghar train station. I had no idea where we were going next, but I happily followed Swamiji. I would willingly follow him anywhere he wanted to take me. I knew deep in my heart that no misfortune could ever befall us.

Liberating the Departed

"We will go to Gaya," Swamiji told me one morning. So we took a train at nine that night from Jasodi Station, and both of us found seats by the window. I was apprehensive about our destination. "The Gaya pandas[22] are very corrupt. Who knows what may happen?" I thought. The train started moving. I do not remember the exact hour it happened, but I believe it was around midnight when Swamiji suddenly said to me in a quiet voice, "Sushil, look out the window."

The train was going at full speed as I peered out into the darkness. To my horror I saw a disembodied human hand, its palm upturned and fingers beckoning toward Swamiji, as if asking him for something. In my sheer fright I stood up. At that moment I was not thinking of ghosts or anything. I was sure it was a real person clinging to the window from the outside, asking for help. I quickly opened the window, but saw nothing that remotely resembled the hand. So I told myself that I had imagined it. Or perhaps, I thought, I had seen saw a gunda, or bandit, who had now fled. Satisfied with my rationalization, I closed the window.

A little while later, to my great consternation, I had the exact same vision. The same disembodied human hand, with its palm upturned and fingers pointing toward Swamiji, was clearly visible outside the train window. I involuntarily looked at Swamiji; he was in deep meditation.

After a few minutes he opened his eyes and said, "Sushil, in my meditation I saw that a bodiless soul is asking me for something." Swamiji resumed his meditation and opened his eyes again after a few minutes. "That hand belongs to a dead woman. I once knew her in Vrindavan. She has no family, so no one gave her proper funeral rites (the pinda) upon her death. Now she wants me to do this for her when we get to Gaya."

"Swamiji," I asked. "Why are pindas given in Gaya?"

Swamiji told me a wonderful story. Long ago there once lived an asura[23] named Gayasura, who wanted to be immortal. He began a very difficult tapasya and passed long years in this manner. His strength grew to such proportions that the Gods were alarmed. They felt that their celestial abode was under serious threat; they began trying to disrupt Gayasura's tapasya in many ways, but they were not successful. In frustration they approached Lord Vishnu: "Lord, you are our only hope for salvation. Please save us from this dangerous asura. Please destroy this insolent Gayasura!"

Sri Hari listened to their pleas and said, "Gayasura has been performing tapasya to Lord Shiva. He is becoming so powerful by this sadhana that he is about to gain the strength of Lord Shiva himself. If Gayasura is not destroyed, he will become as strong as Lord Shiva."

The Gods requested, "Please destroy him, Lord." Lord Vishnu agreed and the Gods were content and departed.

Some days later Gayasura decided to pluck lotus flowers that floated on the magical ocean of milk for his Shiva Puja. As he gathered the flowers, Gayasura continuously yawned. He could not stop yawning and felt an intoxicating urge to sleep come over him. Then Gayasura become very annoyed at himself. "What is happening to me? I am so fatigued that I can barely even support my body!" Despite all his efforts, Gayasura was unable to ward off his overwhelming desire to go to sleep. He had no idea that

Lord Vishnu had set this trap for him. Gayasura collapsed, his flowers scattered on the ground and he fell fast asleep.

Taking advantage of this opportunity, Vishnu slew Gayasura with his mace. The area where he died is called *Gayakshetra*.[24] As a result of this adharmic[25] act, Vishnu became trapped in Gaya, which is why this place is also called *Vishnukshetra*. Eventually, Pitamaha Brahma performed a yagya to purify the place and set Vishnu free.

Gayakshetra is an area of about ten square miles. It is sacred because of the yagya Brahma performed there. If one does the final rites for the dead at Gaya, the departed soul finds everlasting peace.

Getting back to the subject at hand, Swamiji told me, "We will offer this dead woman's pinda at Gaya so her soul can rest. Then we will do a Brahma yagya."

When we arrived the next morning, Swamiji fulfilled his promise. The fire ceremony lasted for three days. Upon its completion, the world felt quieter. It had been drizzling and countless people had come to watch the yagya. They participated in the ceremony by throwing rice into the sacred flames and chanting the ancient sacred mantras. They had never seen such a yagya. Lord Vishnu himself was sitting in their presence. At the end of the worship, the priests of Gaya gave Swamiji a list of the names of their own departed relatives. They requested Swamiji that whenever he performs the Shraddha ceremony for the departed, he mentions their relations as well. Swamiji readily agreed and gave his blessings to the infamous pandas of Gaya.

Bodhgaya

"Our next destination will be Bodhgaya," Swamiji told me one morning. "Lord Buddha spread his message of peace throughout the world. Let us visit the place where he became enlightened."

We started in Gaya and traveled by bus to Bodhgaya, where we stayed at the Birla Dharmashala. A Japanese gentleman, who introduced himself as Kwo, was also staying there. Soon the three of us began to converse about Lord Buddha. In the course of our exchange, Swamiji began meditating and looked like Lord Buddha himself. It was late in the night when he woke from his meditation.

The next morning after our bath, we visited every single holy site in Bodhgaya. Temples from many different cultures abound there. There were wonderful temples from Japan, Tibet, Thailand, Korea and Sri Lanka, and we visited them all. Finally, we went to the actual tree under which Lord Buddha had himself meditated. Then we returned to our lodgings in the evening.

Soon after returning, I noticed that Swamiji crying. I was puzzled by this. I could not imagine what had moved him to tears, so I asked him.

"Lord Buddha meditated here for many days and his body became a skeleton through his fasting and hardship," he replied. "One day a devoted lady named Sujata fed him a bowl of rice pudding. Lord Buddha enjoyed the taste so much that he attained enlightenment that very night," Swamiji explained. "Sujata is still here. If we practice with sincere devotion, we can find her darshan in Bodhgaya. Tomorrow morning I will perform puja and meditate by the banks of the Niranjana River. I will not leave my asana until Sujata comes."

At the crack of dawn the next morning, we bathed at the banks of the Niranjana River. There were no flowers there to use in our worship, but Swamiji was unperturbed. "We will do our puja and yagya with sand and leaves" he told me. "The yagya will continue until Sujata comes. If you cannot remain with me, return to the Dharamshala. You'll find food in the bazaar."

Although I didn't desire to starve to death on the banks of the river, I was embarrassed to abandon him, and so I stayed with him and watched the yagya commence. The puja went on for the entire day. All we had were leaves and a few sticks of incense. Swamiji drew the yantra in the sand, the sacred symbol which is the seat of the deity, and for each of the mantras of the *Chandi Path*, he placed a dry leaf on the yantra. It was the Krishna Paksha[26] and late in the night the moon had risen high in the sky. I was feeling light-headed from hunger and thirst. I was also scared that Swamiji would stay here until he died, but I knew that God's grace is extraordinary. The whole day and night passed in this manner. Swamiji tirelessly continued his yagya throughout the next day.

As dusk approached, I was almost faint with fatigue. Swamiji was reciting the last mantra of the ninth recitation of the *Chandi* he had performed that day. As he finished, I looked up and saw a Bihari woman, accompanied by her husband and children, approach Swamiji. They bowed before him, touched his feet and the woman said, "Babaji, today is my son's birthday. You have been doing puja all day. I would be very happy if you would kindly accept the food I have brought for you." They set down their plates of offering beside the yantra.

Thereafter two other men came from behind carrying a large pot of food. They also placed their offering in front of Swamiji. We turned around and saw that hundreds of people were sitting silently behind us. People from the nearby villages had seen the dedication with which Swamiji was worshipping and had returned to their homes to prepare prasad.

Swamiji was beside himself with joy, and offered the food to God and ended the yagya with the waters from the river. After distributing the prasad to all who came, he ate the wonderful meal. Then Swamiji began singing and dancing. The whole congregation of village people began to dance with him, and a wondrous feeling of joy inundated everyone who was present.

At that moment Lord Buddha and Swami Satyananda had merged into one being, Buddhananda. The entire village and I were witnesses to the indescribable and ineffable bliss he radiated.

Swamiji offering a village yagya

Regaining My Lost Treasure

From Bodhgaya we went to Vrindaban, where Swamiji became immersed in the bhava of Krishna. Every day he chanted the *Bhagavad Gita*, and the translation that he rendered in English and Bengali is testimony to his understanding of the message of Lord Krishna.

After bidding farewell to Vrindavan, we left for New Delhi. On the first night we slept on the floor of a Shiva temple. The next morning Swamiji began a Shiva Puja in that temple. When the priests of the temple saw Swamiji's puja, they were so impressed that they forgot to do their own pujas. They sat and watched. After Swamiji completed his puja, the priests declared that he was the best Purohit[27] in all of India and requested that he do a three-day puja and recitation in their temple.

Before the priests arrived we had no arrangements for food and lodging, but curiously enough, because of Swamiji's puja, we did not have to worry about that for three days. D.P. Shah, a Member of Parliament from Madhya Pradesh, came to that temple to offer puja. He heard Swamiji's story from the other priests who were present, and then sat down to watch for himself. He was so impressed with Swamiji's knowledge of Sanskrit and Indian culture that he invited us to stay in his house.

After spending three days at the Shiva Temple, we went to a housing complex provided for the Members of Parliament. Mr. Shah welcomed us very graciously and respectfully. His wife and three daughters were very happy to see Swamiji and were eager to hear stories of Hastinapura, the ancient Indian name for New Delhi. Then Swamiji related stories from the entire *Mahabharata*.

He told them so beautifully that the ladies were delighted. The next day Swamiji recited the *Chandi Path* at their house. They had never experienced the *Chandi* this way before. The kind family requested Swamiji to stay at their house whenever he came to Delhi. We stayed with them for nearly a week, and every night many of the other Members of Parliament and their families would come to share in the joyous sat sanghas.[28]

Something curious happened to me at this time. I did not know my way around the city at all; I always followed Swamiji around everywhere. I had told Swamiji that I wanted to go to an underground marketplace named *Palika Bazaar*. Swamiji agreed to take me there. "You will not receive any respect by wearing Western pants and a shirt," he told me. "Wear Indian clothes, a dhoti and kurta. No one will laugh at you. Everyone will respect you because you are with a Sadhak[29] of the Sanatana Dharma."

When we arrived, we saw that it was a very sophisticated marketplace with many foreigners and wealthy Indians walking around. There were also many people dressed in dhoti and kurta like Swamiji and myself. In fact, there were so many people dressed in a white dhoti and kurta that I lost Swamiji! Even after looking for him for a long time, I could not find him. I had no idea where I was and I had no money. I did not know the address of the place we were staying, and thus I could not ask for help. I was almost in tears, but my faith in Swamiji was unwavering. I knew he would not let any harm come to me. He is Shiva incarnate. Shiva is the symbol of kalyan, of welfare, and he would rescue me, because Shiva is a savior.

Not knowing what to do, I began walking aimlessly through the streets, singing a song that Swamiji always sang "Jaya Shiva

Omkara." I walked for two hours, not knowing where I was going, and to my amazement and relief, I found myself at the doorstep of D.P. Shah's house! Swamiji was already there and he embraced me. "Silly boy!" he said on seeing me. "I was meditating for you."

That is how I regained my lost treasure.

Establishing Devaloka Ashram

It was late at night when we got on the train. We found our seats and the train pulled away from the station. Swamiji began to sing, "Jai Chandi, Jai, Jai!" A couple of cranky passengers started protesting about Swamiji's singing, but then everyone became quiet. Swamiji's magical voice intoxicated the passengers with joy and they all went to sleep peacefully. I did not even realize that I had fallen asleep as well. When I awoke, I saw that Swamiji was still singing. Finally the train stopped at Haridwar Station. Nearby passengers touched Swamiji's feet and took his blessings before they disembarked. "You are the living Shiva," they said, and commented that it was the best train journey any of them had ever had.

Holy saints and seers have long come to Rishikesh in furtherance of their spiritual search. Swamiji told me, "This is the same Rishikesh where many rishis performed tapasya and found liberation."

Swamiji and I were both barefoot and clad in knee-length dhotis and shawls. We had a small bag of clothes and books. We walked for some time before reaching the ashram of an old Bengali widow. It was a small ashram made of earth. One of Swamiji's disciples, Somanath, was a nephew of this Mataji.[30] It was he who had given us his aunt's address. Swamiji had educated Somanath, who was born to a poor Brahmin family of a small village, and now had become an advocate of the Supreme Court in New Delhi.

Mataji welcomed us graciously and fed us tea and sweets. The full cup of tea was so hot that I could not even touch it.

Swamiji told me that this was part of our sadhana. "This is how we will have to cope here," he advised me. "We will be required to move beyond our concepts of hot and cold."

After this we went to the banks of the Ganges River. I was deeply moved by the lush beauty of the verdant Himalayan foothills. Swamiji's bliss radiated like a beautiful light. He danced joyously and gloriously, like Shiva, who danced around the worlds. I felt just like Swamiji. Although I had fasted all day, I felt no weakness nor despair. I forgot all about my life at home — my parents, friends, everything and everyone. I, who had never even been outside of our village, Bakreswar, was now in the far distant Himalayas and delirious with blissful joy. This was only possible because of Swamiji's blessings.

Dusk approached and we returned to Mataji's ashram to eat. "I have made sleeping arrangements for you to stay here tonight," she said.

Back at the ashram we met one of Mataji's devotees, Satpal Bali. Satpal Bali touched Swamiji's feet as soon as he laid eyes on him. Then Mataji told Satpal, "This Sahib Sadhu wants to perform a strict sadhana by the banks of the Ganges River. You have a house there. Please accommodate him."

Satpal readily agreed. Swamiji named the house, which is still there today, *Devalok Ashram*, the ashram, or place of refuge of divine reality. The house had one room and a veranda. I was stunned. There were thousands of old tires scattered about the room. There were also bamboo rods, wood and piles of empty rice bags, all kinds of garbage. Swamiji said, "We will spend the night sleeping on the veranda. Our project will commence in the morning. Do not fear, Sushil. There is nothing to fear in the world.

We will stay here and do our sadhana. We will be successful because of our pure love. I can feel it!"

The next morning we woke up at four o'clock and bathed in the river. Swamiji said, "Come, we will do puja now."

Puzzled, I asked, "Where will we do puja? We have no place to sit."

Swamiji smiled, "Today's puja is of a different sort. There is a poster in Howrah station that says 'Cleanliness is next to Godliness.' We will do cleanliness puja today!" Swamiji put on a small cloth and instructed me to wear a gamchha.[31] We emptied the house and hauled away the rubbish in the driveway. We had been fasting the whole day and were sweating profusely. At times I felt like running away from Swamiji!

After about ten hours of hard work, the room was immaculately clean. Swamiji noticed that I was very tired. "Sushil, let us go to the Ganges." Swamiji held my hand and took me to the river as we bathed. He said a mantra under his breath, which ended with *Sarva shanti kara bhava*. To my astonishment I felt completely refreshed after the bath, as if I had slept excellently for hours. Some time later Swamiji said with a smile, "So, do you still want to go home?"

I embraced Swamiji. It felt like I was embracing my mother. There was no fatigue, no fear; only pure bliss and joy. I looked up to see that Bengali Mataji had brought hot tea, samosas and jilebi for us. Swamiji, Mataji and I offered the food to God and then ate with great joy.

Early the next morning we bathed in the Ganges. Mataji and Satpal had arrived at the Devalok Ashram to witness the opening rituals of the fire ceremony. Our quartet surrounded the vedi, the altar upon which Swamiji would establish the fire, and Swamiji began the performance of the Cosmic Puja.[32] It ended in the afternoon. Then Swamiji began the actual fire ceremony. He made the yantra, arranged the wood pieces and welcomed Agni, the God of fire. The fire ceremony went on through the night. "This yagya will end in 108 days," Swamiji told us. Mataji and Satpal returned home very late that night. I fell asleep, but Swamiji continued the ceremony all night long. We had no food except tea in the morning and puffed rice and grilled eggplant, which we made for dinner on a small stove. "This is how things will be for 108 days," said Swamiji. After fifteen and half weeks of this diet, I was surprised to find myself feeling perfectly healthy.

All the inhabitants of our locality were present on the last day of the yagya, as they were eager to receive the great blessings that abound at the end of such an auspicious event. Swamiji made everyone happy by blessing them all.

One childless Sikh couple wept at Swamiji's feet and begged him to bless them with a child. Swamiji gave them a piece of fruit from the fire and instructed, "Eat this and recite the *Chandi Path* every day." One year later they had a son. They are still devotees of Swamiji.

That night Swamiji and I sat across from each other in the room. In the middle of the room we had a very beautiful vedi made by Swamiji himself. Shah Jahan's Taj Mahal would feel ashamed if compared with it. Swamiji told me, "This is a new creation. From today onwards this ashram will be called *Devaloka Ashram*. The Gods will live here. It is because of your sadhana in many previous lives that you will be able to see and participate in this great one hundred and eight day yagya."

I could not help but feel apprehensive: we only had enough money and supplies to last us eight days, but I said nothing to him about my fears. Suddenly Swamiji yelled, "What money are you thinking of? Is this earthly body everything? Even if we die of hunger, this yagya will go on! Brahma, Vishnu and Maheshwara themselves will come to this yagya. And if Vishnu comes, then Mother Lakshmi[33] will also come."

Swamiji began chanting his mantras. I fell asleep and did not even know it. When I woke up at four in the morning, I saw that Swamiji was still sitting in his asana and tirelessly chanting mantras, in preparation for the coming day's yagya. At that precious moment of Brahma Muhurta, the early morning hours when the birds are just beginning to sing and all of creation is waking up, Swamiji spoke so eloquently and with such an immense divine presence that to me, he appeared to be the four-faced Lord Brahma himself. The whole room became a heavenly abode. I even felt Lakshmi Devi's presence.

Many Hindu Punjabi families resided in Rishikesh. A few days before Swamiji's yagya was to end, a Sikh lady came in to see Swamiji. "My husband is an alcoholic and he beats me up. He wastes all his income on liquor. It is very hard for me to raise my children under these circumstances. Please cure my husband so that my family can be saved."

Swamiji said, "If you can bring your husband here on the last day of this yagya, I will try my best to help you."

After she paid her respects to Swamiji and left, a sadhu came in and said, "That woman's husband is an alcoholic and a gunda.[34] Please do not allow him into the ashram. He will do us harm."

Swamiji only smiled in reply. The day the yagya was to end

the Sikh lady came to the ashram and said, "My husband refuses to come here."

Swamiji whispered a mantra into the unhappy lady's ear and said, "Say this mantra at home and you will see that your husband will be amenable to coming here."

At midnight, just as the yagya was about to end, I saw the lady coming into the ashram with a man. I do not know what mantra Swamiji told her, but I saw that the couple came in, bowed their heads and sat at Swamiji's feet. Swamiji marked both their foreheads with the sacred ashes of the homa fire. Several years later that same couple came in to visit the ashram and I was pleasantly surprised to see how things had changed. He was a completely different person. The husband asked Swamiji, "What can I do for you?"

Swamiji replied, "I need nothing. Just love your family and the community. Only then will we find peace."

On the Banks of the Ganga

After the one hundred and eight day yagya was completed in Rishikesh, we decided to go to Haridwar on foot. We completed our pujas at dawn and left the Devalok Ashram by six in the morning. "We will walk alongside the Ganges River all the way to Haridwar," Swamiji explained. A Spanish youth accompanied us. He also wanted to make the same trek. As we walked, Swamiji started singing, "Devi sureshwari, bhagavati gange, tribhuvana tarini, taralo tarange."[35] We joined him in his singing and continued walking without rest.

We arrived at Haridwar before noon. When we reached the holy city, we saw a huge crowd of people by the Ganges, engaged in a festival of worship. Swamiji instructed us to join him and we bathed in the sacred river's waters. After bathing, Swamiji sat on the banks of the river and began his puja. We sat down beside him. Swamiji looked as beautiful as Shiva, and all the participants in the festival came over to watch the puja and began to touch his feet. Many gave him gifts of fruits and sweets. When Swamiji woke from his meditation, the three of us offered the tasty gifts to the Gods and distributed the prasad with great joy. Then Swamiji started chanting, "Gangamaya ki jai!"[36] and all the people began to shout in tune with his chants.

Dusk approached, and I asked Swamiji where we were going next. Swamiji seemed a little impatient with me. "Have I not told you? 'Vasudeva Kutumbakam. The whole world is our family.' Why do you always insist on asking me where we will stay and what we will eat?"

On hearing these words, I realized his wisdom and embraced

Swamiji. We continued on our way. After walking about two kilometers, we arrived at an ashram. It was named Saptarishi Ashram, in honor of the original seven seers of the Vedas: Gautam, Bharadvaja, Visvamitra, Kashyapa, Jamadagni, Vashishtha and Atri. These seven rishis were the first to explain the meaning of dharma through Vedic chanting. Swamiji did a tapasya for these seven holy saints at this ashram.

We sat under a big mango tree by the ashram while Swamiji started his evening prayers. The ashram was very quiet and was located in a remote place near the bank of the Ganges. Due to the power generated by Swamiji's chanting, the surroundings brimmed with life and energy. Hearing the holy mantras, the mother of the ashram, a Belgian woman, graciously invited us to be her guest. She asked us in and her husband, the father of the ashram, a very kind Indian sadhu, joined her in talking with Swamiji. Afterwards we were fed with great kindness and received their generous hospitality. The sadhu of the ashram was also very happy to have us there. After we ate our food, they provided us with comfortable accommodations.

When I woke the next morning, I saw that Swamiji had already bathed and was reciting the *Chandi*. He completed his recitation by nine in the morning. All the disciples of the ashram, the sadhu and his wife placed garlands around Swamiji's neck and together exclaimed, "You are Shiva himself! Your pronunciation of Sanskrit is so wonderful and sincere. Because of your beautiful *Chandi* recitation, the whole ashram is blissfully happy."

Tested by Wind and Water

A Swami named Virananda lived on the bank of the river near Tatipara, a few miles away from Bakreswar. Swamiji stayed with him in his humble hut and chanted the *Chandi Path* every day for one hundred and eight days. They were two sadhus living alone away from civilization, so they wore only loin clothes and ate one meal a day.

The last nine days of their one hundred and eight day vow of worship were the nine days of the Navaratri,[37] the worship of the Divine Mother. Swamiji was radiant. He used to chant from morning to night sitting in one asana. The village people were ecstatic to have Swamiji performing such an intense sadhana in their area. In honor of the Navaratri celebration they constructed a large bamboo frame and attached a tin and canvas roof over the area where Swamiji was worshipping. They even prepared an idol of the Goddess Durga slaying the buffalo demon Mahishasura, and requested that Swamiji perform the installation ceremonies for this deity of their community's worship. Then every day the whole village went out to the bank of the river where the two sadhus were performing puja, and they joined in the celebration.

Pachu and I, along with some of the other disciples, stayed with them for the nine days of Navaratri. We woke up at three in the morning and took a bath, then we did arati, chanted the *Chandi Path* and did a homa. At five in the afternoon, when our chanting was completed, we performed the evening arati. After arati all the disciples ate their one daily meal, while Swamiji fasted the entire nine days. (I have actually seen him fast on only water for forty days on several occasions.)

On the eighth day of Navaratri, Swamiji was chanting alone in the pandal.[38] Suddenly a great storm came over the mountain. The wind and rains came down so violently that everyone ran into the sadhu's hut for shelter. It was a small mud hut with a tile roof, but the walls were thick and the roof was well constructed. There was hardly any room inside for all of us. The wind was howling and the sound of the rain was ferocious. We closed the shutters tightly and were all too scared to even peep outside. It felt like anyone who ventured outside would be blown away. It is amazing that, in all of this, no one even thought of Swamiji.

A few hours later the storm finally passed and one brave soul ventured to crack open the door. When we looked out through the open door, we found that the entire structure of the temple that the villagers had made for Swamiji's worship had collapsed. There wasn't a pole standing, and all the tins lay strewn in a heap of canvas and bamboo. What a mess! Then it occurred to us, "Where's Swamiji?"

"He must have fled to safety when the storm hit," said one disciple.

Another suggested, "Maybe he outran the storm and made it back to Bakreswar."

Someone else said, "What about the pratima, the idol of worship? I wonder if the altar is still there."

"Let's go see," was the consensus.

Slowly we braved the perils of the muddy fields, sloshing across the embankments of the rice paddies towards the bank of the river, towards the heaps of tin, canvas and bamboo. As we approached the heap we heard chanting coming from inside.

"That must be Swamiji! Quickly uncover this mess!"

We all started to lift the tins and untangle the bamboo, and when we pulled away the canvas and got to the bottom, much to our amazement, we found Swamiji still sitting in his asana, still reciting the *Chandi Path*. He looked around at all of us with a great smile, and then said the "Pranam," the closing mantras of the recitation. Then he passed me the book in his hand and stood up. He was soaking wet from head to toe, and there was a large cut across his back, where the sharp edge of the falling roof tin had cut his skin as it came crashing upon him. But he was radiant with light. He slowly walked to the hut, took off his wet clothes and wrapped himself in a blanket. He laid down on his straw mat without saying a word, looked up at the ceiling and smiled. He just lay there smiling until late at night. Soon we all got hungry, so we left him alone in his reverie with the other swami, and returned to our homes to eat and rest in comfort.

The Divine Mother Arrives

A few weeks later Swamiji decided to sit for another one hundred and eight day worship at another temple in Bakreswar, named *Bhatala*, the great Banyan Tree. Swamiji, Pachu and I went to Bhatala to prepare for his worship. Swamiji told me to lock the gate of this small temple every morning at five and not to open it again until seven in the evening, at which time he was finished with his daily worship. He told me emphatically not to let anyone inside for any purpose without his permission.

So we purchased a large padlock, which I used daily to lock the only entrance to the temple from the outside, and then I threw its only key in through the window to Swamiji. He placed the key by his asana, and when he completed the mantra of his worship in the evening, he threw the key through the window so that we could come inside.

Swamiji was eating only one meal a day, so every evening I brought him his meal, a plate with two rotis (pieces of homemade bread), one cup of dahl and a sweet. He was performing the Cosmic Puja and chanting the *Chandi Path* in various styles and samputs[39] all day long, every day.

Swamiji had prepared an earthen image of the Goddess Kali. In her hand, in the place of the severed head of the demon She had slayed, Swamiji had affixed a cut-out photograph of his own head. One day a constable came to the temple and said to Pachu, "Open the gate. I have heard that there is a foreigner inside, and I want to check his papers and see what he is doing here."

"I'm sorry, Sir," replied Pachu. "He has the only key and he is not going to stop chanting until the evening when he finishes the last mantra. I am not able to open the door."

The constable seemed disturbed by Pachu's answer, but left the village by the last bus.

About a week later the constable returned along with an inspector in a jeep and their driver. The inspector said to Pachu, "Open the gate. We want to see what the foreigner inside is doing and check his papers."

Pachu replied, "You can look through the window and see what he is doing. He has been chanting the *Chandi* all day long every day since Kali Puja, and he has every intention of continuing through Shiva Ratri."

"Well, tell him to open the gate and let us in to talk with him," said the inspector.

"You can tell him anything you want through the window, but I am sure he is not going to acknowledge your presence or answer you until he finishes chanting."

"When will that be?" asked the inspector.

"After seven o'clock at night," Pachu replied.

So the inspector left.

Another week went by and one day, late in the afternoon, two police jeeps arrived with an escort: two drivers, two constables, the inspector and the Superintendent of Police. All had come to the little temple where Swamiji was chanting. We were all terrified. What were they going to do to our Swamiji? They stood outside the window of the temple and listened to his chanting. About an hour passed until Swamiji finished the last mantra of his recitation. He lit a kerosene lantern, reached for the key and threw it to us outside the window. We opened the door and brought him his food, and the Superintendent of Police and the inspector came in behind us. When they saw how respectfully we entered the temple, they stopped and removed their shoes, and then very politely entered into the small village temple where Swamiji was worshipping. The superintendent went immediately to the altar where the lantern was shining brightly. He looked at the artistry of the image that Swamiji had crafted from clay with his own hands, and then stopped in amazement when he saw the picture of the severed head of Swamiji in the hand of Kali. He looked at the photograph and looked at Swamiji, then looked at the photograph again. He turned to the inspector and said, "This man knows something. Leave him alone!"

He touched Swamiji's feet and said, "You will never have any difficulty with your passport or visa as long as I am in this district. If anyone asks to see you papers, tell them to come to me."

He bowed politely and exited. The inspector also bowed and touched Swamiji's feet and left. From that time onward, Swamiji never had any difficulty with his visa or passport in the north of India.

One day I went to town to go to the big market there, and I gave the key to Pachu. That was the day Shree Maa and her disciples first came to the temple. On arriving, Shree Maa said to Pachu, "We want to go inside."

Pachu replied, "No, Mother. No one can go inside without Swamiji's permission. I will ask him if it is okay."

Pachu entered the gate and went to Swamiji and said, "A Mataji[40] has come and would like to come into the temple for a minute. She is really radiant, like a great sadhika,[41] and it would be nice if she could have darshan."

Shree Maa

Just then Swamiji noticed that Pachu had left the door ajar, and a whole bunch of people were entering through the open door. They went into the temple and sat down and began to meditate. Swamiji became angry with Pachu. "You know I am not seeing anyone," he raged. "Now I am going to be late for my worship! Get those people out of here so I can begin my puja!"

"How can I get them out?" asked Pachu. "They are meditating in a Hindu temple. That's why we make temples. So people can come to meditate."

Swamiji was getting more and more angry. Still no one moved from the temple. After about forty-five minutes he finally went to the temple door. He began to clear his throat and make funny noises. One of the men from the group finally rose and came outside. "Oh, you are a foreigner!" he called. "Have you had a chance to see all the famous sites in India? Have you seen the Taj Mahal?" he inquired.

"What are you talking about?" stammered Swamiji. "Why are you talking about the Taj Mahal? I've got my sadhana to do. Get out of here! You're wasting my time!"

Then all the people left the temple. They were all well-dressed city people. They certainly weren't from our village. Swamiji calmed down and addressed them more politely. "Please excuse me. I haven't completed my worship yet, so I have no prasad to offer you. If you go to the temple across from the bathing tank, they have much prasad to share. Please leave me to my worship. I really don't want to be disturbed."

Suddenly the group parted and Shree Maa came out of the temple. She walked between the two lines of devotees and right up to Swamiji, and put a flower on his head, a sweet in his mouth and stood there looking him in the eye. She was radiant, with a little stream of tears flowing down her cheeks. He looked at her with amazement. She was the form of Kali that he had been worshipping. After years of worship, the Divine Mother herself had come to his ashram, and he had just yelled at her entourage telling them to get out, telling them they were wasting his time. He looked at her with complete absorption, and then she suddenly turned and walked away. All the devotees followed her through the gate, and Pachu closed the gate and locked it from the outside.

Everyone stood at the little window and watched Swamiji's puja from the outside. His worship was so succinct, it seemed as though he had just had the darshan of the Divine Mother. They stood there watching him at least until mid-day, and then they left Bakreswar.

At night when I came with food, Swamiji said, "A Mother came to our temple today. She is a Divine Mataji, so beautiful and radiant. Where did she come from? Try to find out who she is and where she lives. I want to know more about her."

That night I asked everyone about the visitors to our village. No one knew anything about them. Some people said they came from Calcutta. Nobody knew who they were or precisely where they were from. I returned to Swamiji the next day with no information to report.

After Swamiji had completed his sankalpa,[42] we made food for the priests of the temples and the poor people. We invited all the people of the village for rice pudding that Swamiji had prepared himself. Swamiji had some money at that time, so he also gave each of the Brahmin priests a piece of cloth and ten rupees. He fed about two hundred people that day, and made them all very happy.

Feeding the village children

In Search of the Divine Mother

It was some time later that I learned the rest of the story directly from Swamiji, which I will now tell you. Having completed his sankalpa, Swamiji had taken the train to Calcutta en route to Gauhati in Assam, where he wanted to worship at the Kamakhya Temple. When he arrived in Calcutta, he got down from the train at Dakshineshwar and went straight to Ramakrishna's room, where he sat in long ecstatic meditation. In his meditation he heard the word *Belgachia,* and he went outside and asked someone in Hindi, "What is the meaning of *Belgachia?*"

The man replied, "*Bel* means 'fruit' and *gach* means 'tree.' *Belgachia* means 'fruit tree.'"

That didn't mean much to Swamiji, so he went to bathe in the Ganges. While he was changing his clothes on the steps leading down to the river, a portly Bengali man was also changing his clothes nearby. Swamiji asked him in Bengali, "What is the meaning of *Belgachia?*"

The man replied in Bengali, "*Bel* means 'fruit' and *gach* means 'tree.' *Belgachia* means 'fruit tree.'"

Swamiji asked again, "Do you know of any special fruit trees by that name?"

"No," replied the Bengali man. "But there is a bus stop with that name."

Swamiji thanked him and immediately went to the bus stand. "I would like a ticket to Belgachia," he said.

"Which one?" replied the ticket collector. "There are two Belgachias. One is on this side of the river, and the other is on that side."

"I want a ticket for the Belgachia on this side of the river," replied Swamiji.

The collector responded, "The stop is over there. The bus just left. The next one will be here in about an hour."

"Where is the bus to the Belgachia on the other side of the river?" he asked.

"It is over there," he replied pointing. "They are just boarding."

So he went to the Howrah bus and purchased a ticket to Belgachia. He told the collector to please tell him when he got there because he wouldn't recognize the stop, and so he went across the bridge, and drove down toward Howrah. After about forty minutes, the ticket collector came and said, "This is Belgachia."

He got down from the bus and found there were three roads connected to a circle. In the center of the circle was a little island, and in the middle of the roundabout was a fruit tree. Of course there were a number of rickshaws around the fruit tree. Some of the drivers came over to him and asked him, "Where do you want to go?"

Not really knowing how to answer, Swamiji suddenly remembered the Divine Mother, who he had been worshipping for the last fifteen years and said, "Where is Maa?"

One of the rickshaw drivers replied, "Maa is everywhere!"

Swamiji didn't know quite what he was looking for, or really where he was going. "I want to see Maa," he said.

The rickshawwala[43] called the youngest of the drivers and said in his Bhojpuri language, "You've got a great fare here. Take him on a tour of the city, and show him a temple of Kali."

Swamiji didn't even ask him the fare. He sat in the rickshaw, and traveled up one alley and down another. He explored every bump in the road of the whole Belgachia suburb. That rickshawwala took him out to the farthest edge of the community to a little tiny Kali temple, far away from the main bazaar, and there he stopped.

Swamiji said to him, "Please wait here."

Inside the temple there was a small statue of Kali. The pujari appeared astounded to see him, and immediately gave Swamiji a tilak, or spot of red powder over the third eye, and a blessing, and was waiting for an offering. He gave Swamiji some holy water and asked, "Do you speak Bengali?"

"Yes," was the reply.

He said, "May I ask you a question? This is the most amazing thing. All of the foreigners who come to Calcutta go to Belur Math. They go to Dakshineshwar and Kali Ghat. How did you happen to come to this temple? You are the first foreigner ever to come here."

"I am looking for Maa," Swamiji replied.

"Do you mean Shree Maa?" he asked incredulously.

"Of course I mean Shree Maa," came the reply. "Why would I search for a Maa who isn't the respected mother? Of course, I am looking for Shree Maa."

"She is in that house across the street," the pujari said pointing.

Swamiji still didn't understand what he was being told. He didn't know Shree Maa's name was Shree Maa, nor could he imagine who it was that he was about to meet.

He told the rickshaw driver to wait, walked across the street and knocked on the door.

Suddenly the door opened and a little old man with long white hair and a flowing white beard tied at the base of his chin grabbed him. He was one of the men who he had seen at the temple in Bakreswar. The man hugged him and dragged him inside exclaiming, "She said you would come! She said you would come!"

Swamiji went into the house, which was filled with people singing kirtan, songs about God. When they saw him enter, they all lit up and sat up straight.

"Maa has been meditating in her room on the roof since yes-

terday," explained a man named Vashishta. "We have all been waiting for her darshan, but she hasn't come down from her room yet. She's been sitting in the same posture for more than twenty-four hours, and hasn't eaten anything at all. She hasn't moved for any reason. She has just been sitting in the same place without the slightest movement. But now that you are here, she will surely come down!" he said emphatically.

He escorted Swamiji to the temple in his house. Less than ten minutes later, Shree Maa came down the stairs and entered the temple. She was the same Divine Mother that Swamiji had seen that day in Bakreswar. They just sat there looking at each other, and had a very profound and deep meditation. Ever since that moment, Swamiji has been traveling around the world with Shree Maa, conducting programs and festivals of worship.

Finding Work for the Destitute

The first time Swamiji brought Shree Maa to stay with us in Bakreswar, I acted rather strangely. I was an unemployed gradu-ate (like thousands of others), my father was ill and my family was experiencing severe financial hardships. Immediately after their arrival, I pointed my finger at Shree Maa, right in her face, and in a very familiar, informal village-slang style of Bengali said to her, "Are you going to help me get a job or not?"

Shree Maa spoke very little then, and usually just sat with her eyes closed. So she was not used to receiving and responding to questions, let alone such an abrupt and demanding request. In response, she suddenly opened her eyes and said, "My blessings are always with you. You have a lot of work to do."

I wondered what she was talking about, but did not press the matter any further. A few days later Swamiji invited me to go with them to Calcutta, where they were to perform a yagya at the Sunrise School on the Howrah side of the river, across from Calcutta. Instruction was given in English at the school, and be-cause of Shree Maa's and Swamiji's work on their behalf, the school had been accredited by the Government of West Bengal.

Swamiji organized all the materials for the yagya and was just about to start when I arrived. Around the sacrificial altar sat some of the most important people in both the school district and the government's education departments. The Secretary of Edu-cation was even present, as well as a number of principals of area schools and other government officials.

Swamiji seemed to be hesitating to begin the ceremony and everyone was waiting. Suddenly he looked up and said, "I can't begin this auspicious fire ceremony until we find a job for this young man here!" He pointed to me and everyone looked at me and then back towards Swamiji, as if they were trying to understand exactly what the relationship between the two of us was. He was a foreign sannyasi and I was a village Brahmin. What were we doing together, and why couldn't he start the fire ceremony without my being employed? Clearly he had started numerous other yagyas without my having a job. What was so imperative about the present yagya and the present circumstances?

And then, to my amazement, Prasadji, the school's owner, stood up and said, "I will give him a job! Start the yagya!"

Swamiji smiled in reply and began his recitation of the invocation of the fire as though nothing unusual had happened. I sat in total amazement, wondering what kind of job, what kind of salary and what kind of karma I had performed in a past life to have made such a devoted friend who would even receive an invitation to perform an auspicious yagya in front of such a distinguished assembly, let alone tell them that I, a village Brahmin, must have employment before he would start. God is indeed wonderful!

And that is how I became a Sanskrit teacher at the Sunrise English Medium High School of Belur in Howrah.

Bringing Peace to Bamangachi

Prabir Mitra had often asked Shree Maa and Swamiji to reside with him at his flat in the Bamangachi Railway Quarters near Calcutta. When I became employed in Howrah, Swamiji agreed and invited me to live with them. So I had a beautiful flat to stay in just a few miles away from Sunrise High School, where I worked. I lived with Shree Maa and Swamiji in a residence in which sat sangha was going on around the clock. I taught Sanskrit at the school for a few hours every day and spent the rest of the day with my Gurus.

I was fortunate to have no expenses, as Swamiji took care of everything. Shree Maa bought me clothes and cooked for me, there was no rent and all I needed was enough money to pay the small bus fare to get to and from the school where I taught. I was able to share in almost constant sat sangha, which brought me immense joy. I felt blessed and as though my life was absolutely divine. I had no idea what I had done to get a job in the city and to be living with my Guru, without expenses, and to have such great karma. I was just a simple village Brahmin with a deep desire to know God. And God, indeed, had blessed me with a wonderful opportunity to do just that!

One day I was drinking tea at a roadside stall. A man named Harudas was sitting next to me. Now Harudas was a notorious thug, but I had nothing personal against him. In fact, I knew that he had helped many people in their times of need. We were making small talk and I was just picking up my cup to take another sip of tea.

Suddenly, seven or eight people from an enemy gang rushed

up to Harudas and grabbed him. Knocking over the tables filled with tea, they wrestled him to the ground. It all happened so fast that no one knew what to do. We were all overcome by surprise and fear. It happened in an instant. And then, in front of my incredulous eyes, they decapitated him. My blood still chills at the memory of his writhing, headless corpse. I still remember the feeling of being showered with fresh human blood and the gore. For days after this atrocious murder, I was unable to eat or sleep. I had known that Bamangachi was an unsafe place, but I had been so glad to have employment and a free place to stay that I had never even thought of such an experience.

After this happened, I became determined to leave Bamangachi and go home to Bakreswar. So I told Shree Maa and Swamiji about the incident. When they heard the story, they both replied, "We must establish peace in Bamangachi." So they told their devotees that they wanted to perform a Chandi Puja at the Bamangachi Railway Quarters Field.

"It is impossible to do a puja there," their devotees responded. "That is the favorite meeting place of our town's most notorious criminals. It's a very unsafe place."

But Swamiji was adamant. "I will do a puja there," he insisted." Bamangachi is in desperate need of peace."

So Swamiji called two of his devotees, Prabir and Tiwariji. "We will go to the artisans at Kumartolli," he told them. "We need to prepare images of the deities Mahakali, Mahalakshmi and Mahasarasvati." They all went together, and Swamiji gave the craftsman very precise instructions on how to make the images. So the men began their work. Within a few days three stunningly beautiful statues of these goddesses had been created.

Swamiji had a devotee there named Hanuman Das Gunda who had been a notorious gang leader. So Swamiji went with Hanuman Das and invited the gang members to the puja. He brought them to the area where the puja was to be performed, and then Swamiji and Shree Maa asked them to protect the worship while it was in progress. "We want to create an atmosphere in which all of your families will feel safe to attend the ceremony," Swamiji told them. They all agreed to help them.

A few days later, they started performing the Spring Vasanti Navaratri Puja. On hearing the excitement and music that was being generated, the townspeople came to watch the worship. Every day the crowds grew bigger and bigger, until by the sixth day all the women of Bamangachi were present. These same women previously would never dare set foot outside their homes to brave the dangers of that notorious town. Yet on the seventh day, the women of Bamangachi assembled in the puja area, danced their hearts out and joyously performed arati together!

On the ninth and last day of the puja, the terrorists of Bamangachi all approached Shree Maa and Swamiji. "This is the best puja we have ever seen," they said. "How can we help you?" Shree Maa and Swamiji replied, "Just make Bamangachi a safe and peaceful place. That is all we want."

That same evening, everyone in town, including the terrorists, went to join the arati. Gang members who had previously been in constant opposition suddenly began to dance together. There were too many people there to count — a sea of joyous human faces, dancing together and celebrating God. And from that time onwards, Bamangachi knew only safety and peace.

Durga Puja Blessings

The principal of the school where I was teaching Sanskrit was a devotee of Shree Maa. At that time the school was of average size and had no special status in the community. One day Shree Maa went to the principal and said, "Your school needs a Durga Puja." Delighted to be offered such an unexpected good blessing, the principal, Prasadji, heartily agreed and invited Shree Maa and Swamiji to bless the school with a puja.

So, in the Fall Navaratri of 1982 Shree Maa and Swamiji began a Durga Puja celebration at my school. By the third day of their nine day ceremony, countless people from Howrah, Calcutta and Belur had come to witness the puja. I was fortunate to be there as well.

On the night of the last day, we took the Durga Pratima murti[44] to the Ganges River. Although there were dozens of other murtis there, countless people wanted to see our murti, which had been lovingly made by Shree Maa and Swamiji's own hands and hearts. We all performed evening arati on the banks of the Ganges. Such a sight had never been seen before in all of Calcutta. We danced and sang and the celebration was so joyous. Then we performed visarjana[45] and returned to Prasadji's house. After the puja was complete, the school underwent tremendous, positive changes. It received an award for academic excellence, its team excelled in sports, a planned agitation of the teachers for more money was called off and all the political factions decided to leave the school alone. It is now a well-known and respected institution. In fact, it is now the largest English-language high school on the Howrah side of Calcutta.

Answering My Prayers

I went through many changes after spending so much time with Shree Maa and Swamiji. I am the only son and my parents had feared that I might become a beggar. When I came home in November of 1982 after witnessing the Bamangachi Puja, my parents insisted that I stay with them for ten days. Unbeknownst to me, they had secretly arranged for me to be married. So, soon after I arrived, I met my bride to be and was married! It all happened so quickly that I was unable to inform Shree Maa and Swamiji. I told them of my marriage only after the ceremony. Having been their devoted disciple since my teenage years, I was afraid they would be angry with me for entering the householder life without even discussing it with them.

Shree Maa and Swamiji were staying in the Devalok Ashram. They arrived in Bakreswar a few weeks after my marriage. Immediately upon their arrival, they came to our house and blessed my new bride, Dipali. "How do you feel about Sushil staying with us?" they asked her. "You know he is employed in Calcutta."

"I only have two wishes," replied my new wife. "I want my husband to get a government job so he can be home in Bakreswar, and I want to have a son." Within the year our son, Sourav, was born, but my wife's second wish had not yet been fulfilled. Getting a government job in West Bengal is extremely difficult, next to impossible. As I have experienced time and again, though, Shree Maa and Swamiji's blessings always bring success.

Within a few days of our return to Calcutta, an advertisement appeared in the local newspaper soliciting applications for two hundred new school inspector positions in the Government of

West Bengal Education Department. At the time I was living with Shree Maa and Swamiji at the Bamangachi Railway Quarters. Madhuri Roy Chowdhury, a devotee of Shree Maa, was the head clerk of the West Bengal Government's Education Department. She was a regular visitor to our home. Mrs. Chowdhury suggested that I apply for the position, and Shree Maa and Swamiji heartily agreed.

The requisite qualifications included a Bachelor's Degree in Education, a Master's Degree and three years teaching experience, all of which I had. Thirty thousand candidates applied for the two hundred openings. With Shree Maa's blessings I passed the first hurdle and was called for an interview. My interview and examination were held in Murshidabad, Bharampur. Both my oral and written exam scores were excellent, and far beyond what I had ever dreamed possible. I still never thought, in my wildest imagination, that I would get one of the jobs. Thirty thousand candidates were competing for two hundred positions. It wouldn't be possible to get one of those jobs without paying a heavy bribe. That was how one got hired for government jobs those days.

Soon thereafter Shree Maa and Swamiji, who were then living in the United States, came to India and went to visit Mrs. Chowdhury at the offices of the Department of Education. While they were visiting, they started singing bhajans and then Swamiji began telling stories in his unique charming and engaging style. Suddenly officers began to pour in from the neighboring offices. Everyone was sitting around listening to Swamiji's stories and to Shree Maa's songs of devotion. They were so charmed that some exclaimed, "When we are with both of you, we feel such inspiration. What can we possibly do to help you in your mission?"

Swamiji immediately replied, "One of my disciples is a candidate for one of the school inspector positions. I would love to make sure he gets that job."

Shree Maa said, "His name is Sushil. Please put a red mark beside his name."

Some time later I got the good news that I had been hired. I was the newly appointed School Inspector for the West Bengal Government. My wife's second wish had come true.

When I wrote to Shree Maa and Swamiji in America to tell them the good news, they replied: "Are all your prayers now answered?"

That is how they work their magic wherever they go.

When I first started to visit Swamiji in the cremation grounds on the bank of the Bakreswar River outside our village, I was often ridiculed by many of my classmates. They wore bell-bottomed trousers and fancy shirts, smoked cigarettes and talked about movie stars. I was just a simple Brahmin pundit, clothed in homespun traditional Indian dress, and spent all my free time with this foreign sadhu who resided in the village's cremation grounds. Only the "untouchables" and the dead spent time in the cremation grounds, and not necessarily willingly.

More than thirty years have passed since those days of my youth, and I am now the fifth highest ranking government official in our district. The same individuals who used to laugh at me when we were young boys now regularly visit me to ask for help in their projects. And it's my great joy to offer them whatever help I can provide!

Panchavati Forest Yagya

"We have created a wonderful new community here," Shree Maa and Swamiji wrote me once from California. "We would love you to join us, Sushil." Despite my best efforts, it would take me fourteen years from that first invitation to finally make it to America. I had to wait for them to come to India instead.

I was thus really happy when, in December of 1992, Shree Maa and Swamiji, along with twenty-five of their disciples, came to Calcutta and stayed at the Meera Mandir. When I went to pay my long-awaited respects to my beloved Gurus, I was fortunate to meet some of their new disciples.

First, we all went to see the Dakshineshwar Kali Temple, where we spent the entire day chanting and doing puja. We also went to Kalighat, the famous temple of the Goddes Kali, where Swamiji had often performed pujas. Earlier that day, during her meditation, Shree Maa had received a vision of her beloved Guru, Thakur Ramakrishna. He had told her: "Swami Satyananda should do a yagya at the Panchavati forest in Dakshineshwar." Because of the strict rules of the trust set up after Ramakrishna's death that governed that forest, no one since Ramakrishna had been allowed to do a yagya there. Getting through the red tape that the trust had created made it difficult to obtain the necessary permission, and our request was turned down for five consecutive days. But Maa was determined to fulfill Ramakrishna's request, as revealed in her vision. Finally, after much persistence, the secretary of the Dakshineshwar Temple gave in and granted us the permission.

It was the day before Amavasya, the dark night of the moon.

During the evening, Maa asked us to make all the arrangements necessary to begin the yagya the next day, on the new moon. So everything was prepared that very night, and at six o'clock the following morning we all congregated at the Dakshineshwar Temple. The altar had been lovingly prepared and was really beautiful. Our puja commenced at six-thirty, and the yagya followed at nine in the morning and continued throughout the day, ending at five in the evening. All the inhabitants of Dakshineshwar had joined us by that time. On hearing our ecstatic worship, they had come to receive the blessings of the yagya. Shree Maa and Swamiji gave everyone who came a tilak[46] on their forehead and a blessing. We had fulfilled Ramakrishna's wish and all felt very satisfied.

Calming the Terrorists

Shree Maa and Swamiji were traveling in South India when an insurrection broke out in Assam. "We must do a puja at Gauhati," Maa said to Swamiji one day. "Terrorists are torturing many innocent people."

So Shree Maa and Swamiji left South India and went to Gauhati. They stayed at the home of Dr. Chakravarty, and arrangements were made for a large Durga Puja there. Dr. Chakravarty himself sent me a kind invitation to join Shree Maa and Swamiji for the Durga Puja at his home. A large tent was erected in the field behind his house, within which an image of the Goddess was installed and a large havan kund was built upon which to invoke the deities of the fire. Shree Maa and Swamiji led the worship for nine days, and the crowd of participants grew larger every day. By the eighth night of worship people had brought huge railway ties to burn in the sacred fire, and hundreds of people were making offerings into the fire while thousands were chanting the mantras.

When Swamiji began the arati, the crowd was wild with joy! He offered all of the implements, while the other participants were singing and dancing. Then he took a bell and began to ring it. The rhythm became faster and faster. He handed the bell to someone else who maintained the rhythm that he had played, and then he took a drum. He played the drum for a while, then handed it to someone else, and he took a tambourine. He played the tambourine for a while, then handed it to someone else, and in this way he played many instruments, increasing the rhythm of the chant as he went along, and passing the instruments off to others to continue playing. After he had played every instrument in the orchestra, the only part he had not yet played was that of the Divine Mother. Swamiji went over to the altar of worship, sat down in meditation before the image of the Divine Mother, and merged into samadhi.

It was early in the morning before Swamiji awoke from his samadhi. Hundreds of people, who had spent the night watching him, were still present when he awoke from his beatific state. Everyone bowed before Shree Maa and Swamiji and asked for their blessings. Many of the terrorists had come to the puja and touched the feet of the visiting saints. After this Durga Puja peace returned to Assam.

Circle of Peace

Swamiji had once told me, "Sushil, we will hold onto the hands of all the children of the whole world. We will all join hands and make a beautiful circle of peace. You will see that this circle has endless bliss. It will be the face of society's bliss and happiness." I did not believe his words at the time. We have now stepped into 2000 AD. On New Year's day, Shree Maa, Swamiji, Suratha, Adyananda, Laloo, Siddhananda and I were all together at Malikarjuna Temple on Shrisailam Mountain in Southern India. On that day Swamiji said to me, "Sushil, it is now time for you to come to America and go on tour with us and see for yourself how dharma is manifesting in the western countries. Hold hands with your brothers and sisters, new and old. The circle of peace is unbelievable."

Sushil Choudhury telling stories about Swamiji

My First Trip to America

On April tenth of the year 2000, I left my home and reached Varanasi to join Swamiji, Shree Maa and their disciples. The next morning we all gave puja to the Goddess Annapurna. Shree Maa and Swamiji were completing the Navaratri Puja. I arrived on the last day. At this Annapurna Mandir, the puja began at two in the morning and ended four hours later at six. Then the yagya commenced and finished around noon. Countless people came to see this beautiful puja. No one had ever seen such a puja here before.

Navaratri ended on April fourteenth. We reached Delhi on April fifteenth. That night we stayed at a five star hotel. Devanath was my roommate. We hardly slept that night; we just stayed up talking for hours. The next morning we began a ritual of our own: reciting the *Chandi Path* together. We then did pranam to Shree Maa and Swamiji. That evening Sanjay, another disciple, arrived with our dinner, lovingly prepared by Shree Maa.

After dinner we all went to the Indira Gandhi International Airport. I felt an indescribably delightful sense of anticipation. This was my first trip on an airplane. I had never even been inside an airport before. At eleven at night I sat in my seat on the Singapore Airline flight. I was one of twelve, including Shree Maa and Swamiji.

The next morning we reached Singapore. After some rest our plane arrived in South Korea. We rested there for an hour and then flew for the whole night, until we reached San Francisco Airport the next afternoon. Devapriya (Devanath's wife) and Ashish Goel picked us up from the airport and took us straight to the Devi Mandir in Napa, California. My life-long acquaintance and journey with Swamiji finally culminated at this point: I was now in his temple in America. Parvati, Kamala and Gautam greeted us at the Mandir and put garlands around our necks. We spent five happy days in the Mandir.

On April twenty-second we began our tour around the United States. The sincerity of the people here, and the joy in their worship, fills me with joy. Wherever we go, we meet with people who are not only practicing dharma, but are living it. The delights I am experiencing on this tour will take another book to describe. I offer my deepest love and respect to the feet of Shree Maa and Swamiji, and my fondest love to all of my brothers and sisters, new and old.

Hayley as an American Kumari

Shree Maa's Stories

Meeting Swamiji

One night the Divine Mother woke me suddenly from samadhi with the words, "Go to Bakreswar and meet Satyananda." When I came out of samadhi I told those who were with me at the time about my vision. Those days, people's names would come to me during samadhi, and then they would come to see me. So when I mentioned the name, *Satyananda,* one of my devotees

replied, "Oh Mother, Satyananda will come to see you. You don't have to go to him."

But when I later went back into samadhi, the same voice again instructed me to go to Bakreswar and meet Satyananda. Then I saw a vision of Swamiji coming down from heaven. His two hands were raised in blessing, and he was chanting the "Devi Suktam" from the *Chandi.* He floated down through the air and went before the Shiva statue, and then merged into this idol of worship. On seeing this, I knew he was a divine man and that we must have some important karma together.

When I woke from my meditation I said, "I have to go to Bakreswar. Where is Bakreswar?"

One of my devotees replied, "I know where it is. It's near Calcutta. There is a famous Mother temple there."

So a week later we went to Calcutta. In Calcutta we took a bus to Bakreswar, arriving at our destination in the evening. As soon as we found a place to stay, I sat down and went into meditation to get guidance from the Divine Mother. I sat in samadhi the whole night. The next morning I woke up out of my trance, and the Divine Mother's energy was pulling me. It was so powerful that it forced me to start running. I ran through the temple grounds like a wild woman until I reached a small temple at the far side of the temple complex, underneath a large banyan tree. There I saw a man opening a lock to the gate of that modest temple. I told him I would like to see Satyananda.

He ran inside and said to Swamiji, "You have to see this Mother. She is something special!"

While they were talking, I noticed that the man had neglected to lock the gate behind him, so I went inside to meditate, joined by about twenty people who were with me. After more than half an hour, I heard a man's voice say, "Get those people out of here!"

I woke up out of samadhi and took a marigold flower and a sweet, and went to see that man. On coming outside from the temple, I recognized Swamiji from the vision I had in my meditation while at the temple in Kamakhaya. I put the flower on his head. We looked at each other. Tears were flowing down our cheeks. I put the sweet in his mouth, and looked again. And then I walked out, not even turning around once to look back at him. That afternoon I returned to Calcutta.

I knew he would come to find me in Calcutta. I waited patiently, knowing the Divine Mother would show him the way to me, just as She had shown me the way to where he was. I later learned that he had completed a one hundred and eight day vow to chant the *Chandi* and perform daily worship of the Divine Mother every day in that small temple where I first saw him, never allowing himself to even leave the small confines of that tiny, modest temple. That is why it took him so long to find me. The bramachari who had been at the gate had brought him his food and water, and thus enabled him to remain in seclusion and perform this constant worship.

It was a few weeks later, while I was in Vashishta's house, sitting in samadhi, that he finally found me. I remained in samadhi at Vashishta's for two days. My devotees were worrying over me, "We have to interrupt her samadhi or she will leave her body," they were saying, according to a common Indian understanding that if a saint stays away from the body for too long, then she will not be able to re-enter it. They were all chanting loudly, with great devotion, because they wanted to wake me up out of samadhi. There was a big group, perhaps fifty or sixty people. On the third day I woke up out of my samadhi sometime after noon. It was at that moment that Swamiji had come. I could feel that he had come. Vashishta was downstairs hugging him and crying, "She said you would come! She said you would come!" I heard him say, "She's upstairs in samadhi. She has been like that for two days. But she knows everything. She must know you are here. I am sure she will come down!"

Swamiji replied, "She will come down." He took his seat in the temple. A few minutes later, I went downstairs to meet him. And that was how it all started.

Lots of miracles started happening once I met Swamiji. We

started performing big pujas with thousands of people in attendance. It seemed like all of Calcutta came to worship with us. We traveled together to so many different places: Bangladesh, the Himalayas, Nepal, all over India. I wanted to wake everybody up, and he was the most engaging pujari any of us had ever seen. He would sit the entire day and perform sadhana. He explained mantras with so much bhava, with so much divine inspiration, that everyone who met him knew he was a great rishi, a sage who embodied and spoke true wisdom. When he told stories, everyone felt like they had been transported back to Vedic times, and were there themselves, directly experiencing the great teachings of the Vedic rishis. When he chanted, he lost himself for hours at a time. He would sit in one asana for the entire day. And when he would meditate, he went into the deepest samadhi. Within a very short time, his face would glow with divine light.

Many people would attend Shree Maa and Swamiji's pujas

My "Foreign" Pujari

Swamiji and I used to travel throughout India visiting temples. Whenever we went to a temple, it was our custom to perform puja, chant and do as much sadhana as possible in these holy places. Swamiji would usually perform the puja and the sacred fire ceremony, while I would sit in meditation beside him, or accompany him with the offerings. Often I went into samadhi. Often he did too. That was our life. We would chant and sing, and then go into the deepest meditation.

Once, we were doing puja in a well-known temple in Benares when a group of Brahmin pandits came to me and asked, "Why are you letting a foreigner perform the worship in your festivals? Shouldn't you honor our traditions and let an Indian Brahmin pandit do your pujas?"

I replied without hesitation, "When you can do puja as perfectly as Swamiji, I will be pleased to take you with me."

Completely Absorbed in the Divine Mother

It was the monsoon season and we were in the Himalayas performing nine days of worship in Julai Jageshwar, in Almora District. I had been with Swamiji for a few years by that time and was in the habit of going into samadhi to support his sadhana whenever he performed great tapasya. He would chant for the entire day, and stay up sitting by the fire for most of the night. Swamiji always slept very little.

We were staying in a mud hut next to the Shiva temple. Swamiji had been performing homa all day long, sitting in front of the fire and chanting the *Chandi* forwards and backwards from morning until night. Because it was the rainy season, Swamiji had placed the green wood all around the fire pit so it would dry out and could be used for later homas.

I was meditating on a cot to support his sadhana. I had been deep in samadhi for about five or six hours when suddenly my body felt like it was burning up. When I opened my eyes, I saw that all the wood around Swamiji's fire pit had caught on fire, yet Swamiji was sitting as still as a rock, with his eyes closed and a big smile on his face, while chanting loudly and throwing grains into the fire. He was completely unaware that everything around him was in flames. Then I saw that his clothing was on fire, yet he just sat there, completely absorbed in his worship of the Divine Mother. As brightly as the fire burned, so much louder did his chanting become.

I jumped up and wrapped him in a blanket, smothering the flames that were starting to engulf his entire body. Then I poured water over the wood on the outside of the havan kund, the sacred fire pit, which had caught on fire. Swamiji just kept on chanting, never worrying about his personal safety nor the danger he had faced, determined only to fulfill his vow and finish his worship.

When he had finished his chanting, Swamiji stood up and discovered that only a small portion of his loin cloth was left intact on his body. The rest of his clothes had burned in the fire. Fortunately, there were no burns on his skin. That Swamiji was saved from harm did not surprise me. His one-pointed focus while worshipping the Divine Mother in the form of *Chandi* has always been exemplary. How could She not protect her child, who ceaselessly displayed such intense love and unwavering devotion?

Swamiji showing the mudra of wisdom while establishing the letters of the mantra in his fingers

A True Sadhu

In the summer of 1982 we were staying in Janakpur, a small town in the Nepal terrai not far from the Indian border. Swamiji was then doing a sadhana of chanting the *Devi Bhagavatam*, a collection of stories about the Divine Mother, in the Sita Temple located beside Sita Kund, a large pond where the locals went to bathe.

It was summer time and very hot. So every afternoon, after he had finished his chanting, Swami walked to the edge of the pond, seated himself in the full lotus posture and floated out onto the water. People came from all the ashrams in the area to see him. Caring little about all the attention he was generating from his tapasya, Swami stayed in the lotus posture on top of the water for a few hours at a time. People stood on the shore and looked at him with astonishment, but he never paid them any attention. He closed his eyes. His right foot was placed upon his left thigh, and his left foot was placed upon his right thigh, and with his backbone completely straight, he floated upon the water.

From the moment the Divine Mother gave me my first vision in samadhi of Swamiji, I knew he was a great sadhu. The more time I spend with him, the more I am delighted by the unending variety of austerities he performs to worship the Divine Mother. He constantly finds ways of demonstrating the sincerity of his love by choosing the most challenging practices from ascetic tradtions. I have seen him sit naked in the snow as well as in the hottest of waters. I have seen him carry a heavy load of cement to the top of a mountain while joyously singing bhajans. Swamiji's tapasya is not a show he puts on for a few minutes to puff up his ego and display his prowess to all who come, as many so-called sadhus are known to do in India. It is a natural part of his daily worship. It is one of the ways he tests, solidifies and strengthens his devotion to God.

In recent years, I have often seen him sit the entire night in front of a bank of computers while translating scriptures from Sanskrit. This is part of his tapasya in America – one-pointed focus on making the techniques of worship of God easily accessible to all who desire to perform them. He doesn't try to bind anyone to any sectarian practice. He has translated scriptures for every branch of Sanskrit literature. There is no modern rishi more prolific than he. In addition to his many translations, he has written books of History and Philosophy and even of Sanskrit grammar. His behavior has always exemplified what it means to be a sadhu: He is efficient in his every action.

Swamiji reciting the Chandi Path *in a glacial lake*

Sharing the Love of the Divine Mother

One time in Maligaon, a small community outside of Gauhati in Assam, Swamiji was leading a group of devotees in worship during Navaratri, the twice-yearly nine-day worship of the Divine Mother. By the eighth day, he had both shown and taught such discipline in worship that everyone who was participating was proud to be involved. There were doctors, lawyers, all sorts of professionals and their families, people who would not normally follow the advice on disciplined worship offered by a sadhu, nor the teachings of a foreigner, let alone someone who was both.

A crowd of people had been gathering to witness Swamiji's nine-day puja, which had been growing in intensity. The crowd now numbered in the thousands. It extended back across the field where we had set up our makeshift temple as far as we could see. We were sitting together by the havan fire, which was growing bigger by the minute as four men started laying huge railway ties across the burning fire pit.

The roar of the sound emanating from that huge crowd kept growing louder and louder as more and more people got swept up in the ecstasy of chanting the mantras of worship. Several hundred people were sitting around the bonfire burning in the middle of that field, and at least a few thousand more were chanting along with us in the darkness. It's hard to imagine what it is like to have thousands of people chanting the same mantra in unison before the sacred fire.

When the nine days of worship was to end, Swamiji found that he couldn't bear to put out the fire. Once he had shouted out the last mantra, the thought of stopping was inconceivable. So he went to the top of the list of mantras for chanting that night and started over again. The feeling in the crowd was electric. Thousands of people were chanting, hundreds were throwing rice and grains into the fire, and the fire was immense. The vibrations of the chanting and the unity of the group sent a thrill through everyone who was there. It was the experience of a lifetime – one big mass of humanity crying out their love for the Divine Mother in unison.

Once we had completed the entire round of mantras a second time, Swamiji began the final arati. It was unbelievable! Swamiji was ringing a large brass bell, and a group of drummers were beating their hearts out. Then everyone started dancing, and it seemed the night would never end. As far as you could see across that immense field, people were dancing and shouting, "Jai Maa! Victory to the Divine Mother!"

Then Swamiji lifted up his bell and began to ring it loudly and joyously. He handed it to the first person he saw and showed him how to ring it. Then he picked up a gong and started to beat it. He handed it to the next person he saw and showed him how to beat it. He kept picking up instruments, playing them for a while, and then passing them off to others as an invitation for them to join in the music-making. Once he had played every instrument in sight, and had played every part in the orchestra, the only part left for him to play was that of the Divine Mother. So he sat at the foot of her altar and went into samadhi. His face was aglow, his body luminescent.

It was late in the night when he sat down, yet it wasn't until the first light of dawn fell on his unwavering form that he woke up. On coming back to this world, he first swirled his tongue around his mouth to gather what little moisture was left and to moisten his throat, as most sadhus must do upon returning from samadhi. Because they are not swallowing, the mouth stops producing saliva so it drys out, not to mention that he was parched by nine full days and nights of wild and ecstatic chanting by the roaring fire and from having fasted on only one glass of water a day for the entire nine days, as is his practice.

Then he slowly opened his eyes. There were still a few hundred people left, who had sat with him through the entire night just to be in his presence. Some were meditating; others were sitting in quiet reverie. Most were just watching and waiting to see what would happen next.

Seeing how parched he looked, I offered Swamiji a glass of water to try to quench some of his thirst. He took a few sips and then finished the entire glass. Then he looked up at the assembly and smiled gently. It was then that all in attendance knew he had just returned from his wonderful communion with God.

The Palm Reader

Swamiji knew every path in the Himalayas. I was quite concerned about our safety when he first took me there, but everywhere we went people greeted him with open arms and offered us their generous hospitality. He often sat in temples and read the *Chandi Path.* Sometimes he took a break and read people's palms. There was always a line of people hanging around, waiting for Swamiji to get up from his asana and start seeing people. I once asked him how he learned to read palms, and he related the following wonderful story.

I was walking from Ranikhet to Karnaprayag on my way to Badrinath one time. I came down from a mountain path and crossed a one-lane motor road, deciding to follow the road for a short piece of the journey until I found another village path that would offer a shortcut through the mountains to Karnaprayag. After a few miles, I saw a most amazing site. I had never seen such a thing while walking in the mountains. There was a line of cars parked by the side of the road. There were so many cars that there was barely enough room for other vehicles to pass, and all the drivers were sitting by their cars chatting away idly. I walked up to a few of them and asked what was going on.

They replied, "Don't you know? Namkeen Baba is establishing a new temple in the forest near here. People have come from all over: Delhi, Bombay, Lucknow, Calcutta. The path to the temple is over there," they said pointing.

I couldn't imagine who Namkeen Baba was or what kind of temple he was establishing, so I decided I'd better have a look. I walked up the path and was surprised to see coolies carrying whole bedding mattresses on their heads up the steep incline towards the top of the mountain. Large ladies, dressed in their city finest, were waddling up the mountain side. I was growing more and more curious about what could possibly be going on.

When I got to the top of the mountain, which was a few miles away, I looked down into the next valley and saw an entire encampment. There were thousands of people down in the valley, sitting and talking on blankets or mattresses, bathing in the river, and generally milling about. In the center of this throng of people was a little bamboo shed with a straw roof, open on all four sides, decorated with banana stalks. In the middle of the shed under the shade, a short, fat old man sat on a charpai, a bedframe strung with rope, and he was smoking a big water pipe.

Everyone was crowding around trying to get close to his shed. Left of the hut, near the riverbank, a group of sadhus were seated around a fire, smoking ganja in chillum pipes. Not far from them was a large kitchen area, with twenty-four fires aligned in military style in two neat rows. There were three men attending to each fire, upon which thirty-six gallon drums were being used to cook for what must have been at least 25,000 people camped in the valley.

I immediately went to join the sadhus, as was my custom, and greeted everyone, put down my things, and went to bathe in the river. I returned to a waiting cup of tea, and then a chillum pipe made its rounds around the fire and we all traded stories until dinner came. Sadhus are always served first, so we didn't have to wait to eat and after cleaning up we went to bed early.

In the morning all the sadhus woke up long before the first light of dawn, took our baths and returned to find our fire blazing brightly. It was very warm by the fire, which took away the chill from our cold river bath. Someone made tea, and after the first light of dawn, I sat down to recite the *Chandi Path*. I completed my sadhana for the morning, and then went over to where the crowd was gathered around the bamboo shed.

There were a lot of people, but because I was a sadhu and a foreigner, and because of God's grace, somehow they thought that I had greater authority to be there. People just kept stepping out of my way and pushing me forward. It didn't take much time for me to reach the thatched shelter. The line of people wanting to have their palms read just kept coming. I walked alongside the line, bowed to the Baba with respect and sat down at the foot of his bed. He was reading someone's hand. I sat there watching. It was fascinating.

He said to a village man in Hindi, "Tomar nehin hoga. (It won't happen.)"

I asked, "Where did you see that?"

He turned to me and asked, "Tum kaun ho? (Who are you?)"

I introduced myself and then asked him where he was looking to see that the anticipated event wouldn't happen. He showed me. I kept asking him questions and he kept answering. All kinds of people came to ask him for advice: politicians, farmers, business-men, housewives, rich and poor. Everyone wanted to know what the future would bring.

Finally he asked me, "Don't you want me to see your hand?"

I said, "No. I just want to see how you see other people's hands."

"Bhaite raho. (Stay seated.)" he said.

I didn't even notice that I had spent the entire day watching him read palms. They called me for dinner, and I got up to eat. One day led into the next until I spent almost five months with Namkeen Baba. We walked through the mountains together with his little band of sadhus, and stopped at every village we came to. Everywhere we stopped, they immediately brought a rope bed for Babaji to sit on. Someone would fill his water pipe with tombac, a very astringent mountain-grown tobacco, and a line would form immediately for people to show their hands and seek his counsel.

He knew every herb and root in the forest. He was a great homeopathic doctor, and he freely distributed medicines and herbs to those who needed them, or told people where to go to find them. He was not pretentious in any way – a very humble man who everyone treated like his or her own grandfather. He never took money. He just read palms and gave people wise advice.

So Swamiji read palms, and told people about the wonderful effects of performing yogic exercises, pujas and meditation in their lives. He never counseled anyone to wear a ring or a gemstone, as was common practice for palm readers and astrologers. When people asked what they could do to improve their lives, he always told them that the *Devi Bhagavatam* proclaims, "The Gods get their powers from drinking the nectar of devotion, the rishis get their powers from performing tapasya and the ashuras get their powers from wearing stones or amulets. We don't want ashuric powers. What we want has nothing to do with the outside. We want changes to take place on the inside." It is for this reason that he never recommended gemstones.

The Divine Mother's Red Cloth

Every year we traveled together to the Kamakhya Temple in Kamrup, Assam for the festival celebrating the Divine Mother's menstrual period. Swamiji performed large yagyas outside the temple during the three days the temple was closed. Every year before the temple is closed, it is the custom of the temple priests to wrap the statue of the Divine Mother in a white cotton sari. Then they lock the temple gates and everyone stays outside for three days to allow the Divine Mother to enjoy privacy and peace during her menstruation.

Outside the temple the worshippers sing and chant and perform various kinds of sadhana. Once the three days have passed, the priests reopen the temple, only to find that the white cloth that the Goddess had been wearing has turned red. They take this *Rakta Vastra* (red cloth) and transform it into a sacred symbol of the Divine Mother's power and compassion. To do this, they cut the red cloth into small strips and distribute it to the sadhus, who in turn prepare amulets from the cloth to give to their disciples.

Gopal Sharma was the chief priest of the temple at that time, and every year he gave Swamiji an extra large piece of sacred red cloth. Swamiji then performed a special puja while preparing amulets from the Kamakhya Rakta Vastra. Swamiji has even translated several portions of the *Kamakhya Tantra*, the scriptural text that contains the mantras for preparing these amulets, as well as many other secrets of the Goddess. Whenever Swamiji chanted the *Kamakhya Tantra* in the Kamakhya Temple, all the temple priests listened silently, with great devotion. Swamiji was always well loved and well respected in Kamakhya.

Teaching about Hinduism

The Muslim League once invited us to attend a function in Bangladesh. All the most learned scholars of Islam were cross-examining Swamiji on the meaning of Hinduism. They couldn't understand how an educated man from a country like the United States could accept a religion containing what they considered to be the foolishness of Hinduism. Swamiji was not disheartened. He held his ground and patiently answered each of their questions.

His answers in both Bengali and English were so succinct that the chief priest said,

"You should go to every village in our country and talk about the meaning of Hinduism. You have taken the philosophy and culture of Hinduism and made it relevant to modern life. If our people could share your understanding, it would be very helpful in building bridges between our Hindu and Muslim brothers.

"As Muslims we are not really adhering to the tenets of our faith. Like Hinduism, our practices have also become corrupted, and thus even most Muslims do not understand the real meaning of Islam, just as most Hindus do not share in the vision of universality that you have explained so beautifully. All religions need people like you to keep their inspiration alive. Please travel around our country and share your wisdom."

The Power of Prayer

There were many wonderful things that I saw with Swamiji. He always fasted for the nine days of Navaratri, four times a year. He fasted forty days on only drinking water on more occasions than I can count. At one time, he stopped talking for six months. The intensity of his worship, the inspiration his talks provided, the energy that he conveyed to groups of people — all make me believe that he came to this earth with a divine purpose.

When I stayed with him in his ashram in Rishikesh, I met many of his old friends. They told me stories of what it was like to have a friend like Swami Satyananda. They told me stories of the days when he was a young Swami traveling barefoot through the Himalayas. He loved the Kumaon region, and spent much time walking the length and breadth of the mountain areas in Pithoragarh, Naini Tal, Almora and Garwal. In those days he traveled on foot to the most remote places.

Swami Vireshwarananda Giri once related the following story of Swamiji's travels in Himachal Pradesh:

Swamiji was doing sadhana in Himachal Pradesh, a high mountainous region in the far north of India. He was traveling on foot following a trail that went alongside the Spiti River. The sides of the canyon he was traversing rose higher and higher as he made his way up the river valley. The water rushed even faster as the valley became more narrow.

After a few days of hiking, he finally reached an area dominated by large boulders and took a detour that went up the side of the mountain. He climbed higher and higher until he entered the forest, and then the path narrowed until it appeared to be only an animal track leading into the wilds. Swamiji followed the track until he reached the edge of a glacier. As was often his habit, Swamiji was walking barefoot. Brambles and thorns had become frozen in the ice he was crossing. The only way to traverse the glacier was to walk upon these thorns with his bare feet.

Once he had started on this path, he knew he wouldn't be able to turn back. The only way out lay ahead of him. The animal track by which he had come led between thick brush, and in that direction it was at least a few days walk before he could find a path to a human habitat. He was almost out of provisions, so he needed to cross this treacherous glacier.

His feet froze quickly and became numb, so he couldn't feel them, yet he saw a trail of fresh blood oozing from the cuts and scratches he endured with every footstep. It wasn't long until his feet became so caked with blood that they turned completely red.

There he was in the middle of the glacier, totally exhausted, hungry, tired, with his feet cut to shreds, leaving a trail of fresh red blood across the frozen white expanse. His steps slowed as he lost all sensation in his feet, yet he continued to make his way across the ice to the far edge of the glacier. Once he had finally crossed the glacier, a journey that took an entire day, he looked ahead and gasped. He stood at the edge of a precipice, before a great waterfall that roared down several hundred feet to pound on huge boulders and collect in a mountain lake.

Imagine the despair he must have felt at this moment. His feet were torn to shreds and so frozen he could barely walk. Behind him was a hike of several days, back across the glacier of frozen thorns and through a Himalayan forest. In front of him was an enormous waterfall, dropping into an unknown valley. And the sun was about to go down. He had no food and one lightweight blanket. It was miserable.

There was no wood at that high altitude, so he had nothing to burn to keep himself warm through the night, nothing to eat to ease his hunger and one thin blanket to protect him. His feet were covered with blood, and he was faced with the inevitable trial of having to climb down the face of a frozen waterfall in the dark.

So he did the only thing he knew to do when all else failed — he prayed. He sat down on the ice, wrapped himself in his blanket and started to sing. He sang all night, even though his teeth were chattering and his body was shivering all over. He sang every Sanskrit hymn he had ever learned. He recited the entire 700 verses of the *Chandi*, which he had memorized. He chanted, performed japa and sang, doing all he could to keep from falling asleep on that remote glacier during the cold Himalayan night, knowing he might not survive until morning if he didn't stay awake.

When at last the dawn came, Swamiji began his arduous descent down the face of the waterfall. He moved very slowly and carefully from rock to crevice, working his way down into the valley below. It was almost midday when he reached the valley floor, and with great delight at having survived the ordeal, he took off his clothes and washed in the river. It had been two days since he had eaten anything, and he felt weak and tired. His feet were a mess, too sensitive to touch and too painful to walk any distance. But he had no choice. So he slowly began to walk from rock to rock down the river valley. After a few hours the valley broadened out, and he found a footpath alongside the river. He was overjoyed to be walking on plain earth! No frozen thorns, no ice, no boulders. Just the soft earth of a Himalayan river valley, and the warmth of the sun's rays as they illuminated the valley.

He continued his slow and painful trek for another hour, never knowing when his legs would give out or if he would collapse in exhaustion. But then, in the distance, he saw the most glorious sight! A lone man was walking up the footpath in his direction. He estimated the man was about a half-hour away. Excited to finally see someone after his three-day ordeal, Swamiji gathered what little energy he had left and quickened his pace.

The figure was slowly approaching him on the trail. In short order he was only fifty yards away. Yet he offered no greeting; he made no sign of having even seen him. Swamiji waited until he was a little closer, and then with folded hands he called loudly in exuberant greeting, "Namaste, I bow to the God within you!"

The man looked straight into Swamiji's face, let out a

horrified scream, and turned and ran back down that same path as fast as his legs would carry him.

Swamiji was overcome with exhaustion. He was tired, hungry, badly in need of medical attention and his one chance of finding help in this deplorable situation in a most remote corner of the high Himalayas had screamed in terror and ran away from him on first sight. What was the problem? He wondered what would happen next. What if he wasn't able to make it to the end of the path? And what would greet him when he arrived there, if he did? So he sat down and took rest, and tried to gather his energy for the next phase of the journey. It seemed he had no other choice but to keep on walking.

After an hour or so, he got up and walked some more. A few more hours past. Then he saw them coming up the trail. A whole group of them. Village men and farmers, carrying sticks, pitch forks, all kinds of implements with sharp points. They were walking fast and carrying these implements like weapons, holding them in an angry and threatening posture. They were headed up the path, headed straight for Swamiji. When they were only twenty yards away, Swamiji did the only thing he knew to do when all else failed — he prayed. He sat down in the middle of the path, took up his meditation posture and began to recite Sanskrit mantras, especially the hymns to the Goddess from the *Chandi*: *Namastasyai, Namastasyai, Namo Namah* (I bow to you, I bow to you, I bow, I bow).

They stopped in their path and looked at him. He continued to sing.

Then they started talking among themselves in their village language. Swamiji kept on chanting. Ultimately one farmer turned and went back down the path. The others stood their ground, holding their weapons at the offensive. Swamiji kept on chanting.

A little more than an hour passed. The sun went down, and it was starting to get cold. It was almost dark. Then two men came walking up the path and joined the others. They all talked for a while, as Swamiji watched their every move, trying to understand what they were saying, having never heard their village language before, watchful for the gesture that might warn him if they were about to attack him. All the while, he never stopped his chanting. Then one of the new arrivals approached and asked, "Ap Hindi bolte hain? (Can you speak Hindi?)"

Hearing the first words he had understood since first meeting these villagers, a very relieved Swamiji stopped his chanting to reply, "Yes."

"How did you get here?" he asked.

"I crossed the glacier and climbed down the waterfall," Swamiji replied.

"What were you doing on the glacier in the first place?" he asked.

Swamiji said, "I have been meditating in the forest for several months. I was following the river and lost my way. Ultimately I ended up crossing the glacier, and took the only path I could find to climb down by the face of the waterfall."

The man bowed down to Swamiji, "Please forgive

us. These men thought you were a ghost. They have never seen anyone as white as you, and they couldn't imagine how you had gotten here. No one from the outside has ever come to this valley before. They were ready to kill you. In fact, not knowing how to talk with you, or what to do with you, they sent for me. I am the school teacher in the next village. I am the only member of our tribe who has ever been outside this valley, and the only one who speaks Hindi."

He turned to the other villagers and in his mountain tongue said, "He is not a ghost. He is a rishi. He has been meditating in the mountains and has lost his way. Now we must show him our hospitality."

The men immediately bowed down to Swamiji, as did the school teacher. Then they lifted Swamiji up and carried him to their village. They brought him clean clothes, bandaged his feet, prepared him a delicious meal, and sang and danced throughout the night to honor their holy guest. Swamiji stayed with them for three weeks until his feet had healed, he was well rested and his strength had returned. When he departed, the villagers were very sad to lose the company of the great white rishi, the Sahib Sadhu, who had been sent down from the waterfall, like Shiva, to bless them.

Lakshman's Stories

Swamiji the Storyteller

He was sitting in a tea stall in Bageshwar, in the Himalayan foothills, telling a story. He seemed to be speaking many languages at once, and when he saw me he immediately said something in French. I don't know how he knew I was French. I had been walking down the main street of town. There was only one street. Suddenly a man came up to me and said in English, "One of your countrymen is sitting in a shop up the road." So I walked over to see. In those days it was very rare to see a western man traveling in the remote villages of the Himalayas, so I figured he must be an interesting character. I had no idea how interesting he would turn out to be.

He was telling a story in several languages. He weaved the languages in and out so that everyone could understand what he was saying. It was outright comical. Everyone was laughing and enjoying. He was so poised, so animated, so comfortable in so many languages, and everyone seemed to be listening with intent. When he finished the story he asked me in Hindi, "Chai pyenge? Will you drink tea?"

I said that I would, and in a few moments a freshly brewed cup of tea appeared before me. We became friends very quickly. Then I followed him back to the Shiva Temple where he was staying at the bank of the river. He invited me to stay with him. I stayed with him for six months, until my visa ran out and it was time for me to return to my own country. But I remember that time spent with Swamiji as though it was yesterday.

Walking with Swamiji

We walked from Bageshwar to Baijnath, spent a few days worshipping the Shiva Lingam at the holy pilgrimage place, and then walked up to Gwaldam. Swamiji always tried to keep off the paved motor road as much as he could. Wherever possible, he took the village paths through the mountains and along the rivers, rather than walking along the motor roads. We stopped in every temple along the way. Sometimes he chanted the *Chandi*, other times he sang from other scriptures. He walked with such a sense of surety, such confidence, such a glow of joy and delight, as if it was impossible for any harm to come to him. He used to tell me, "Every tree is doing the mantra with me. Every tree in the forest is holding out their limbs in blessing. How can we come to any harm out here?"

When we stopped he didn't just make a fire. He invoked the fire. He drew a yantra and invited the fire according to the ancient systems of worship. Then he took out his tea pot and filled it with water. He never slept more than four hours in a day. He was always sitting when I awoke in the morning. His puja was so sincere, so full of joy. He sang the mantras loudly, and you could tell he understood every syllable of what he was saying, and was saying it directly to whomever he was praying.

Late one afternoon we were walking together to Karnaprayag. We crossed the bridge and went to the Shiva Temple, down by the confluence of the Alakananda and Pindari Rivers. There was a large Pipal tree there, around which an ancient vedi had been constructed. Swamiji had stayed there many times before. We slept on the cement platform underneath the tree. In the morning we woke up to bathe in the river, and then went to the tea stall next to the bridge for our morning refreshment. In the Ram Temple across the way, some people had just begun reciting the *Sundar Kanda*. Swamiji wandered across the street and sat down to join them. He started to chant with them, and in a few minutes he took the lead. He became lost in the chant, changing the tunes, weaving different verses in and out. Everyone was enthralled, especially with the amount of energy he put into his chanting. After that, the village people couldn't do enough for us.

Vedas versus Ganja

One night we traveled to Gangolihat. There was a Shiva Temple down beside the river. We sat down in the temple and a few men came from the village. Swamiji started to talk with them. Swamiji was sharing the wisdom of the Vedas, and he kept reciting verses in Vedic Sanskrit and translating them into Pahari, a mountain dialect of Hindi. The group of men grew larger and everyone was drawn into the wisdom he was sharing. There was so much peace, so much love.

Some time later an old Vairagi sadhu came in. Swamiji greeted him with respect and invited him to sit by the fire the village men had made for us. "I'm not sitting beside any sannyasi!" cried out the old monk as he walked to the far side of the room and sat down before an empty fire pit by himself.

He put his things down, made an asana, sat down and made himself comfortable. "Does anyone over there smoke ganja?" he called, lifting a large plastic bag in his hand.

All at once all the village men stood up from where they were sitting at Swamiji's fire and crossed the temple to sit before the other sadhu's fire pit. Some men scooped up a handful of the burning logs in front of Swamiji and placed them in the fire pit in front of the Vairagi baba. They all joined in the smoking, and Swamiji was left alone.

He looked deeply into himself, thinking about the attracting power of tamo guna, the power of darkness. Here at Swami's fire was the wisdom of the Vedas. There the other sadhu was offering the intoxication of ganja. And all the men went to the other fire. Swamiji was left alone. He closed his eyes and went into samadhi.

His meditation was so deep, his light so bright.

It was some hours later when he woke up. He moved his tongue around his mouth to moisten the inside and get the juices flowing again. When he opened his eyes, he saw all the men had returned and were sitting in front of his fire watching him in meditation. All the men agreed that they had seen many sadhus come through their village before, but they had never seen anyone like Swamiji.

A Shiva Lingam, the symbol of God

The ghats of the Ganges in Benares

Shankaracharya's Message

I was fortunate to travel with Swamiji to Badrinath, one of the northernmost towns in the Garhwal Himalayas, near the border of China at an elevation of 11,000 feet, to which tens of thousands of Hindus make pilgrimage ever year to receive blessings at the Badri Narayana Temple. It was there that Swamiji did tapasya before the gaddi of Shankaracharya, the seat where the great Guru gave discourse. The image of Shankara was located behind the main shrine of Badrinath. On seeing this divine image, Swamiji made his asana in front of it and went into samadhi.

He was there the entire day, sitting in one posture of meditation, so still that, from a distance, he looked like a statue himself. When he finally arose from meditation, his face was glowing with divine light. He told me that he had spent those hours of samadhi with Shankaracharya himself. Shankaracharya had said, "You must go down to the plains below and share this ancient wisdom with all who desire to learn."

Being in Badrinath with Swamiji was exquisite for another reason as well: Vina Gopala. Vina Gopala was an old man who woke up the deity of Badrinath every morning at four by playing morning ragas on the sitar. Swamiji sat in the scalding waters of the hot springs by the side of the Alakananda River while listening to his sitar music. Vina Gopala sat wrapped in a long quilted coat, with only his face and fingertips exposed. He played his music into a microphone, and it was broadcast through speakers on top of the temple. His ragas resonated from the temple, traveled across the Alakananda River, hit the side of the Himalayan glacier across the river, bounced off the mountain, and echoed back to the glacier on the temple side of the river, reverberating up and down the canyon. It was magical to hear those beautiful ragas resounding through the high peaks of the Himalayas. Those mornings, Swamiji meditated in the hot springs while listening to Gopala's incredible sitar music.

Another time while traveling with Swamiji, we met Swami Dindayala Giri at Vittal Ghat in the Himalayan region near Ranniket. Giriji's ashram is located high above a small river. Swami Satyananda chanted the *Chandi Path* there for one hundred and eight days. It was so remote, and the villagers were so appreciative of Swamiji's sadhana.

Village Greeting

Sadhana in Rishikesh

My most amazing experience with Swamiji occurred when we went to his ashram in Rishikesh. It was nothing like I had ever imagined. His entire ashram was a single room, located inside a half-acre garden, and enclosed by a high brick wall. There was a Shiva temple inside the compound, and the gate to the ashram opened up to the Ganga. On the north wall was an altar with a murti, an image, of the Goddess Chandi and also an image of Kali holding Swamiji's head.

In the center was a havan kund, on the south wall some cooking utensils and food, and the other two walls were lined with books from floor to ceiling. I couldn't even guess how many of them he had written himself! It was incredible that this man, who wandered the Himalayas and sang the *Ramayan,* spoke with such conviction in so many languages, chanted the *Chandi* with such abandon, and performed the sacred fire ceremonies with such joy, that this same Swamiji was such a great scholar and author as well.

But perhaps you have yet to meet Swamiji. Although his skin is white and he looks like a westerner, he dresses in the orange dhoti of a swami, speaks numerous modern and ancient languages, and is as comfortable sitting in front of a bank of computers typesetting text as he is sitting naked on the snows of the Himalayas chanting Vedic scripture. He is no ordinary man. I was so sad when I had to leave him twenty-five years ago, but I am so joyful to have been given the opportunity to share these experiences.

In Rishikesh I did seva for Swamiji during one of his one hundred and eight day chantings of the *Chandi.* That was an experience that changed my life. He started chanting in January on Magh Navaratri and ended in April at the completion of Chaitra Navaratri. His schedule was so regular you could set a watch by his discipline. He rose at four and took a bath in the Ganges. Then he came back to the ashram and sat for meditation. At the break of dawn he gathered flowers from his gardens and performed the Cosmic Puja, the worship of all the Gods and Goddesses. Then he took a short break, rarely more than half an hour.

Once rested, he enkindled the divine homa fire and recited the *Chandi Path* while making offerings at the fire. This recitation took him exactly five hours and forty-five minutes, and I came to know exactly when he was approaching the last mantra. I trained myself to finish preparing our one meal of the day just in time to place the food on the altar precisely at the time he was chanting the last mantra of the *Chandi*. That was my challenge: to be perfectly punctual. He offered the food to God, we did arati and then we sat down and ate.

What a joy! Those days passed by with such reverence! I don't know how many of you have had the privilege of spending time with Swamiji, but how can I describe what a delight it was to share in his worship? He chanted while ringing a bell in each hand. He never broke his asana once he sat down to start his worship. He always sat still with his back straight and his feet intertwined in the siddha asana, a yogic posture used for meditation. He often sat like that for the entire day.

On many days we had visitors, sadhus coming down from their mountain hermitages to escape the cold of winter. He never broke his asana, but gave me strict instructions to attend to all the old friends who came by to share his hospitality. These sadhus all knew Swamiji and had offered their hospitality to him when he went up into the mountains. Now it was Swamiji's privilege to share with them. They always sat in silent meditation at the back of the room behind the fire while Swamiji completed his sadhana. Then they joined us in song and worship, and we shared food. Swamiji's way of life was so full, complete and perfect!

Swamiji performing Yagya

Swami Vireshwarananda Giri's Story

I met Swamiji at Pipal Ghat in Rishikesh, the large pipal tree where the postman came every afternoon to distribute the mail. There was a large cement vedi constructed around the trunk of the tree, and the postman would sit on the platform under the tree and call out the names of the addressees. All the sadhus who had no fixed address had their letters sent to Pipal Ghat, Mayakund, Rishikesh, which was sort of like "care of Postmaster" or "General Delivery." Every time a name was read, at least a half-dozen men came forward to claim the letter, and, after closer examination and some measure of debate, someone claimed the prize. The letter was opened and everyone shared the news of their disciples, friends, families; reported if they had any remarkable news, such as invitations to perform some special puja; or told where they were going to meet their friends on the next pilgrimage.

It is really remarkable that here it is some thirty years later, and many of those same sadhus from under the tree now have their own ashrams, and several of us communicate by e-mail to share the joys of our wonderful life. I met Satyananda under that pipal tree, and we shared some joyous experiences. He was such an energetic man and never wasted a moment. He always had a diary with him and took copious notes on all the conversations he had with any knowledgeable person. He was so eager to learn, and very keen on practice.

I remember the day he came knocking on the door to my room late one afternoon. "Vireshwar," he said, half out of breath. "I just met a great sadhu named Ramdas, whose only possession is the gamcha (thin Indian towel) that he is wearing. He has nothing, travels with no money and is extremely respected by everyone who sees him. He invited me to come with him to Ayodhya for Ram Navami. Do you want to come? We'll be leaving on the evening train."

It had come all too suddenly for me. "I don't have any money to go," I said.

"Neither do I," replied Satyananda. "I'm sure he doesn't either. But I'm going to go to see who this man is, and what he does. He seems to be someone really special."

"All right," I said.

"I'll meet you at the train in an hour," said Swami, and he was off.

We climbed aboard the train in Rishikesh. Ramdas was already lying down across a row of seats when we entered the compartment. He didn't say a word, but pointed up towards the luggage racks, which were empty. We didn't waste a moment, and climbed into the luggage racks and rolled out our blankets. Within a short time we were asleep, and didn't awake until the next morning when the train arrived at Lucknow.

"We'll have to get down here," Ramdas said shaking us out of our slumber.

We jumped down from the top bunks, grabbed our small bundles and made our way to the door. When we reached the platform, Ramdas told us to wait for him by the train to Ayodhya, and he disappeared into the crowd making its way toward the exit.

A few hours had passed and it was coming close to the time when our train would depart. There was no sign of Ramdas. We both became anxious. No Ramdas. There were only a few minutes left before departure. What should we do? After a thorough discussion we decided not to go without him. We didn't know where to go in Ayodhya, we didn't know anybody there, we'd never find our way around. So we decided to go to the front of the station and see if he came.

We walked to the front of the station and sat down on a bench with only a few minutes remaining before the train was supposed to depart. Just as the clock struck the appointed time of departure, three Ambassador cars came rushing to a stop in front of the station. A whole bunch of people piled out of the cars, and Ramdas came last. He sauntered up to where we were sitting and said, "I told you to meet me on the platform by the train."

"When you didn't show up we became worried about you," Satyananda replied.

"I thought we might need some vaccinations," he said, holding out two pieces of paper.

Satyananda took the papers and read while following Ramdas through the station. The papers were official cholera vaccination certificates, signed by the Chief Medical Officer of Lucknow. They both had the name "Swamiji" on them.

One of the devotees had gone ahead to stop the train. He even cleared a path into the very crowded railcar and found a place for Ramdas to sit in a luggage rack. We were jammed onto the seat below, which was crowded with people, and the train departed.

It was about noon, and it was hot. Suddenly the train stopped in the middle of nowhere. All of the people were really uncomfortable. The train was too crowded, the weather was too hot and the train wasn't moving. There was no air, no water, no relief in site. And the train just sat there.

Suddenly Ramdas tapped me on the shoulder from the perch above in the luggage rack where he was sitting. I looked up and he handed me a large, ice-cold juicy orange. I was astounded, and I handed it to Satyananda. Ramdas motioned to Satyananda to pass it on, which he did, and Ramdas handed me another one. One after the other he started passing out these large, cold juicy oranges, as if they had come from a refrigerator. None of us could imagine where these fruits were coming from. He had boarded the train empty handed. He never carried anything with him. There was no way that such a bag of fruit could have been left unattended in the luggage rack, or that anyone would let all of their fruit be distributed throughout the railway car. And there was no explanation of how, on such a hot day, the fruit could have been kept so cold. But everyone in the car got their own orange to eat. They were the sweetest, most juicy oranges that any of us had ever tasted.

Shortly after we had eaten and were refreshed, the train started to move. When we reached Ayodhya, all the passengers were quarantined. Everyone had to be vaccinated for cholera. Ramdas moved to the front of the line; we followed behind him. He showed our vaccination certificates and were immediately released, while the rest of the pilgrims had to wait to be inoculated.

We walked a short distance from the railway station to a large ashram. The Mahanta or abbot of the ashram heard that Ramdas was there and came out himself to meet the visiting saint. After they talked for a short while, we were escorted to a private room, where we bathed, and were fed and lodged with the greatest of hospitality. When we awoke in the morning, we found that Ramdas had disappeared. We went to inquire about him from the Mahanta, but all he could say was, "Chale gaya. (He's gone.)"

Swami Satyananda and I began to roam about the temples of Ayodhya and along the ghats or stairs down by the river. I was thinking about how to find an Anna Kshetra, a refuge for sadhus, where we could get some food. In one temple Swami saw a harmonium, and he asked the priest if he could play it. He sat down and began to sing the *Sundar Kanda*, the Beautiful Chapter from the *Ramayan*, the most famous scripture of Ram, the most famous deity of Ayodhya. Within a short time someone came to join him with a dholak (a village drum) and the beats and the music, and Swamiji's amazing *pranayam* and the incredible style in which he sings the Dohas, all combined into a crescendo of bhava. Within a few minutes a priest brought a microphone and the music was being amplified through loudspeakers. A crowd of pilgrims immediately gathered in the temple and started chanting, clapping, shouting and dancing.

I never saw anyone enlist so much devotion so effortlessly. He seemed to be having the time of his life, and everyone there marveled at the speed and pronunciation and bhava generated by this foreign sadhu. He had learned so many different tunes and different samputs, weaving the mantras of the Ramayan in and out of his song. The devotion was electric, and by the end of the song everyone was lining up for blessings.

After giving blessings to all who were assembled, the priest of the temple invited us for food. He gave us lodging with his family, and asked us to sing in his temple whenever we came to Ayodhya.

In this way we enjoyed the Ram Navami celebrations and experienced the birth of Ram in Ayodhya. Jai Shri Ramji ki! Jai Swami Satyanandaji ki!

Siddhananda's Story

We were traveling in Maharastra on a hot dusty day by jeep. We had stopped at a gas station when two uniformed men came over and started speaking to me and the others in our jeep in what I assumed was the Marathi language. I didn't understand what they were saying, but I didn't like the tone. Swamiji walked over from his jeep to join us and started conversing with the two men.

It didn't take me long to gather that they were trying to extract money from us, a bribe, threatening violence if we didn't comply. Swamiji and the two men walked away from our group while talking. I followed. The tone of Swamiji's voice indicated that we had a problem. He was angry. He asked them, "What do you do for a living?"

He translated their answer to me, "We extract money from people by making them fear for their lives." Swamiji turned to walk away from the men, but they continued to follow him. Swamiji turned to our driver, Sateen, and told him, "Tell these men who we are."

Sateen said to the men, "He is a great holy man. Leave them alone." Yet they continued to ask for money.

Swamiji then told Sateen in a determined voice, "Tell them to bow down!"

Sateen told them, "Bow down!"

They refused. Suddenly, Swamiji lifted his cane over his head above the two men, and yelled at them in a rage, ordering them to bow down, as if threatening to beat them violently. In fear for their lives, they bowed to the ground before him and before the whole group of devotees. After that Swamiji touched each of them on their head with his right hand, whispered some mantras, and blessed them. When they finally rose, Swamiji walked away.

I looked into his eyes as he passed me, and I saw the familiar twinkle and a slight smile on his face, and I knew that the anger and threats were all a bluff. Like a mirror, he had reflected their threatening energy back onto them, making them fear for their own lives instead, and thus had humbled them.

In the winter of 1999 I was with Swamiji in Bimashankar, a Jyoti Lingam or place of pilgrimage for Lord Shiva in West India. A small group of us were traveling around this remote village searching for sadhus. One Guru invited us into his ashram, which he shared with several of his disciples. Swamiji engaged the Guru in a discussion about the types of sadhana that were performing in the ashram, their daily routine and their philosophy on attaining God realization. Swamiji shared with the Guru a brochure describing sacred texts he had translated into English. Everyone was quite impressed, except for one pujari, who inquired, "Well, I see you have authored quite a few books, but what is the extent of your personal experience?"

Swamiji politely, but firmly, answered, "When all the rishis said, 'Neti neti, it is not this and it is not that,' then how can I describe my personal experience? It is beyond definition, something that just cannot be described."

The pujari was not satisfied with the response and began to probe further. At this moment the Guru of the ashram, somewhat embarrassed, said, "It is obvious this man has gone beyond pranayam and meditation!"

The pujari was left speechless and had no further questions.

In the spring of 2000 Shree Maa and Swamiji were asked by the priests of the Annapurna Temple in Benares to perform the *prana pratishtha* ceremony, a discipline that conveys life to the Annapurna deity, during the Spring Navaratri. To my knowledge, no westerner had ever been allowed to even observe this ceremony, let alone perform it himself. Yet the priests of this shakti peeth, a famous place of pilgrimage for the Divine Mother Goddess, had requested Swamiji to perform these most sacred rites for them. Every morning at two thirty, the doors of the temple were opened for Shree Maa, Swamiji and their family of devotees to enter. The doors were then locked behind us, and no one else was allowed to enter until four thirty that morning.

Every day Swamiji performed the abhishek of the deity, bathing the image with milk, yogurt, ghee, honey and sugar, followed by the puja. He started at a different time every morning, depending on what other ceremonies he was performing that day.

At the same point in his puja every day, and at a different time every day, while his eyes were closed and he was performing meditation or doing japa (reciting the mantra of the deity), a man dressed in orange clothes with an orange turban wrapped on his head went up to Swamiji and put a mala (garland of flowers) around his neck and smeared his forehead with ashes. I witnessed this daily for nine consecutive days. On the last day, Swamiji started his puja while the doors were still locked. And yet, even with the doors bolted shut, the same man still came and placed a garland around Swamiji's neck and smeared his forehead with ashes.

After we left the temple and headed back to our rooms that last morning, Shree Maa turned to us and said, "Did you see that man who put ashes on Swamiji's forehead and put a mala around his neck?"

    "Yes," we replied.

    "That man was Shiva."

Jageshwar in the Himalayas

Bhuvananda's Story

Swamiji's daily life at the Devi Mandir is quite miraculous. He is constantly engaged in pujas and ceremonies of worship, yet he maintains such an incredible work schedule as well. The first few years we were here, he did most of the heavy work with a tractor every day. One day he was on a really steep hill. I was in front of the tractor, maybe ten feet ahead of him. He was coming towards me, and suddenly the tractor started to slip sideways, like it was going to turn over on its side and roll down the side of the hill. It was a long way down into the valley. If it rolled it would have meant certain death. Suddenly Swamiji jumped up and put his hand against a tree. He put his hand up and the tractor stopped rolling any further. It just stopped. Just like that.

During the summer of 1997 it was my privilege to join Swamiji and a group of devotees on an outing to a section of the Sierras that I love very much. The area lies on a divide at 9000 feet and provides a view of many snow-capped mountain peaks, forests, meadows and several small lakes. We set up our camp on a meadow alongside a small pond at the base of a large snow drift. A large Shiva Lingam was constructed out of snow for worship. We sat around a homa fire and chanted mantras before the lingam. In the morning, we hiked to some scenic locations and sat in the shade of a small grove of trees surrounded by wildflowers. It was the perfect atmosphere to gather together for sat sangha. The time passed all too quickly. We enjoyed warm sunny days the whole time.

Babu's Story

The first time I saw Swamiji, he looked like all the other American guys who were being called "swami," like all those who dressed up in orange robes and claimed to be wise men. I was thinking, "OK, he's a guy who wants to be holy, a "wanna-be" swami. And it's OK, it's nice to see somebody who's trying to make that effort. All the sects have their set of swamis — the Siddha Yoga group has their set of swamis, and the Maharishis and so many sects. All right, he's the Devi Mandir Swami, or at least a man who wants to be a swami. He's even trying to look very happy like a swami. But I was thinking, "This man has no idea what he is doing. He's just there because he's there."

Of course, Shree Maa, on the other hand, the very first time I heard the sound of her voice, it was like... (he looks to heaven with a deep sigh). When we went up for blessings, I was telling myself, "OK, Maa is OK. I'll bow down, touch her feet and get her blessings." But I said to myself, "I don't have to bow down to Swamiji, and you know, it's OK not to do it, because Shree Maa is the Guru and he's just like everybody else.

But as I got to spend more time with them, I kept getting pulled into the whole Devi Mandir family. I don't know how it happened; it just happened. That first time that I saw him in India, especially, and had the opportunity to watch him closely, to really observe him, it was something like when the *Titanic* hit that iceberg and went down. You barely know the iceberg is there and what you see shows you little of its totality. You cannot even imagine by seeing the tip what is under there. He's the whole Ocean of Knowledge. He's the whole ocean basically. And it's so vast, you can just go in any direction, and it just extends and extends — right from the slums of Calcutta to remote Himalayan villages to Silicon Valley, to every point in creation.

So many times when he was telling stories, he would look at me and ask, "Isn't that right?" I would just look at him and say, "I don't know." With every interaction my head just sank deeper towards his feet.

In the end I started to think maybe I was the "wanna-be."

I see so many people going through that same experience every time they meet him and start to test him. Every time they test him, I grow in my experience, because I learn something new. When he speaks it's not like someone who went to graduate school and "studied" the Vedas — it's the Truth Itself descending. And you can evaluate his teachings from every aspect of judgment: through logic, through fact and through your best intuitive understanding. It's almost like the perfect explanation of anything you ask him.

He has so many different sides, so many forms of manifestation. He's so sweet and gentle and tactful, and then very suddenly, he can be the absolute opposite.

It's just amazing to watch him. The idea of his being white, an American sadhu, and his being suspect on account of that, just dissolves. When you look at him, his skin color and everything is totally dissolved, and you're looking at the personality beyond the caste, creed and color. You see a human being who is what all the world leaders and people who are working for world peace want to be. He's not the physical self, he's that one universal personality common to the whole world.

I still remember his face from the first time I saw him across

the room in 1998, and then how I see him now. I can just feel the
two different pictures in my head. I wonder, "Did I really think
like that about him back then? Because I can't even imagine thinking that now."

It is pretty amazing. I still feel like laughing about it.

Swami performing arati

Parvati's Story: A Bridge from Man to God

Before meeting Swamiji I had no idea that life could be so much fun. I never realized that I could actually take charge of my own life and not have to ride on the fluctuating waves of the mind, dancing between pleasure and pain. It is true that we cannot escape the wheel of birth and death, but we can learn to watch the wheel go around. Swamiji shows and blesses us with the knowledge of how to free ourselves from the bonds of egotistical and selfish attachment, which is the root of ignorance and therefore suffering.

I had been searching for the purpose of human existence and a way to deal with life's constant changes for a long time. Although I had attended various religious functions in my youth, I really knew nothing about God. In search of more knowledge I visited a few different teachers from various traditions. Although I respected them all (Shree Maa says, "Respect is heaven, respect is liberation."), not one of them sat down with me, on the floor, as Swamiji did. He acted like my best friend. We discussed the meaning and mysteries of life in a simple and straightforward manner. It was in this way that I came to know more about God and the meaning of life, and began to pursue those goals that would bring me closer to Godliness. With his help and teaching, all my previous attachments just fell away, naturally. They no longer held any importance. It became obvious what the next step was going to be — Get my life in order!

I first encountered Swamiji in the backyard of a small house, nestled among a grove of trees, in Clayton, California. He was chanting loudly and ringing a bell. Although totally engaged in his worship, he motioned for me to come over and sit down beside him. In front of me was a bowl of rice mixed with other grains. I could tell from his gestures that he was inviting me to join him in his offerings at the fire.

Of course I could not pronounce the mantras he was saying, but I could at least say *Swaahaa* at the end of each mantra, which I later learned means, "I am One with God," while joining in the offering of grains into the fire. At the end of the ceremony everyone sat quietly for a few moments. It was in those brief moments that for the first time in my entire life I came to understand real peace. At this moment, I came to realize that peace is possible to attain.

One of Swamiji's main teachings is that Mother Nature is constantly dancing, as is Her nature. Change She will and change She must. When we identify with the changes we suffer. When we desperately try to hold on and keep the changes from happening we feel pain. Only when we learn to watch those changes with equilibrium, with the feeling in our hearts and minds that this is the nature of existence, only then do we begin to free ourselves from those actions and reactions, which merely prolong the pain of attachment and sow more seeds of the same.

Over eight hundred years ago there was a great Tibetan Monk named Milarepa. He realized the ultimate goal of existence after performing severe spiritual practices. Milarepa was revered by all and considered to be a great saint. He said of the human condition:

In horror of death, I took to the mountains — again and again I meditated on the uncertainty of the hour of death, capturing the fortress of the deathless unending nature of mind. Now all fear of death is over and done.

In the same light as Milarepa, Swamiji has taken this quote and interpreted it according to his ideal of perfection. For me, this is just one more example of the greatness of Swamiji's attainment.

In honor of life, I took to the mountains — again and again I meditated upon the bliss of being and humankind's inherent ability to perceive it. Then I captured that imperishable essence, and now all fear has vanished.

During the 1960s, Swamji was one of the many westerners who took off for the East in search of true wisdom. He is among the few who, in fact, and gained realization and then returned to share with us the wisdom he attained. Swamiji brought not only the wisdom and devotion he gained through more than twenty years of intensive spiritual practices and direct experience of God, but he also brought the most priceless treasure from the heart of India, the respected and Holy Divine Mother, Shree Maa of Kamakhya, Assam. She is a saint born with the knowledge of God. Together the two have devoted their lives to helping others realize the divinity present in every atom of existence.

Many people look for miracles to increase their faith. For me, just knowing that such a being of Light exists is a miracle. All the knowledge that Swamiji has passed down from the Vedic traditions, all the inner changes that have occurred within myself, within the Devi Mandir family and around the world are miracles in and of themselves.

Swamiji has blessed us with many tools to help us cross this ocean of samsara, the ocean of objects and relationships. He has lovingly translated and transliterated scores of ancient sacred Vedic and Tantric scriptures. These scriptures were cognized and practiced centuries ago by the enlightened sages, who lived in harmony with their own selves as well as with the earth. These texts are extremely rare and beneficial because Swamiji has translated the mantras according to their highest intrinsic meaning, so that through contemplation and recitation we can also achieve the same realization as those ancient seers.

Swamiji's life is a demonstration of his love for Divinity and humanity. If he so desired, Swamiji could be in India right now, sitting under a tree and chanting the *Chandi,* but as he has often said, "To make love grow you have to share it." Not only has he sacrificed his life to God, but he also serves as a constant reminder that God is not far away. God is none other than our own selves. God exists within each atom of existence. Realizing the Supreme Divinity within is possible and not some pie in the sky ideal only for the privileged few or chosen ones. God is for everyone. Swamiji's life is about bridging the gap between humans and God. It is about demonstrating the path of how we humans can become God.

On a daily basis he shows us that the goal of existence — peace in our minds, peace in our hearts and peace beyond — is possible. We can see the evidence of this as we examine the path he took to reach this state of Divine Consciousness. Swamiji encourages us to do the same. When Swamiji first started on his spiritual journey, his Guru told him to increase his asana five minutes every month and to begin to learn how to perform a small puja. He is now able to sit eight to ten hours a day in one asana, and worship at the Cosmic Altar of twelve life-sized deities, the Cosmic Puja, which he has translated. In the same way we can proceed slowly, but surely, transforming our consciousness into the presence of the Supreme Divinity.

Never before have I met an individual soul who is filled with so much enthusiasm and joy. It is apparent in any action he performs, whether he is performing spiritual practices, chanting, singing, driving a tractor, working on the computer, giving a discourse, etc. First and foremost, this kind of joy is born from a seed of inspiration. For me, Swamiji is that seed of inspiration. The inspiration is cultivated on a daily basis through sadhana. In the process, our egotistical attachment and selfishness are transformed into the great radiant Light. We become one with the highest divinity.

When I lived with Swamiji and Shree Maa at the Devi Mandir Temple in Martinez, California, we served dinner to about fifty people every Saturday night. Generally after eating, it was the habit of most people to relax and visit with their friends and family. Swamiji, however, often jumped up quickly, pranced into the kitchen and enthusiastically started to wash the dishes while singing, dancing and chanting the Gayatri mantra out loud. Many people did not realize where Swamiji had gone. A few who did know got up and proceeded to the kitchen. We felt a little ashamed that we had not jumped up from the table first. We could not get Swamiji to stop doing his seva, so we joined in the fun too! Washing dishes had never been so much fun. Before we knew it, the kitchen was sparkling clean. Swamiji inspires us to cultivate this precise kind of enthusiasm towards all the duties of life.

How do we cultivate this enthusiasm and love? We perform sadhana. We chant scriptures. We study words of wisdom. We join together for sat sangha. We offer our negativities to the sacred fire, meditate, sing, and dance whenever possible. We offer our one-pointed attention toward any action we perform in order to maintain the highest respect for all. We set goals and work to attain them.

Shree Maa has said, "Nowadays, there is no one doing intensive sadhana like Swamiji did so many years ago in India." One of the reasons Swamiji has come to this country is to show how to do sadhana, how to pull ourselves out of the muck of materialism and confusion. In India, people grow up with Godliness, and it is not unusual to see people immersed in prayer and chanting. The respect Swamiji receives in the temples in India, which often don't allow westerners to even enter, is truly a delight and is well deserved.

Last year about a dozen devotees and disciples accompanied Shree Maa and Swamiji to India on a sacred pilgrimage to visit temples of Lord Shiva. Whenever we arrived at a temple, at first the priests often had some reservations about allowing us to worship there. Generally, they prefer to remain in control and to perform all the offerings themselves. Swamiji always responded humbly, giving the Brahmin priests copies of his books and then proceeding to the temple, taking his asana and chanting with the authority of truth, while most of us followed suit, chanting along with him. By the time he finished chanting, it was obvious to the temple priests that he had a command of their tradition and mantras far beyond their wildest imagination. It never took them long to realize that he was no ordinary westerner, no ordinary sadhu, and then to bow down to him to show their respect. They were equally amazed to see that he had many followers who he had taught to do the same disciplines of worship.

Outside the temples there were often signs posted that read: "Entrance for Hindus only." According to the true definition, a Hindu is one who abhors violence in every form, who always practices harmonious behavior, who loves wisdom, who respects all teachers of wisdom and practices one-pointed meditation. Such a one may be said to be a Hindu. Being a Hindu has nothing to do with the country of your birth, the color of your skin, or what religion your mother or father practiced. Being a Hindu is an attainment. At first, we were a little surprised that such discrimination existed, but because of our faith we knew we would be allowed inside. In some temples only men were allowed inside the inner chamber. So Swamiji and a few of the others joined in. In one temple, as Swamiji was performing Shiva Puja, two of the priests started to argue rather loudly, which disturbed the peace within. Swamiji got up and left.

Later that morning, Swamiji told us about that in ancient times Brahmin priests were cursed with the inability to maintain the spirit of true devotion and surrender. Swamiji's prayer was that these priests would remember their true nature and renounce greediness. His example served as a reminder of the true dharma.

In one small village we visited, Swamiji and Shree Maa were honored with a spectacular greeting of respect. It was a night I will never forget. We had recently arrived in India and after resting up in Bombay for a few days and visiting many of the temples there, we headed to the remote village of Saap. This was the village where Babu, one of our Indian brothers who was traveling with us, had grown up. His family owned a large estate there, and all the villagers knew and loved them. Their home had been the center of community life for many generations.

The history of Saap is very fascinating, so I'll take a moment to briefly relate it. Centuries ago there was a man who lived in a nearby village who was a cowherd. Every day he went out into the plains with his cows to let them forage. But there was one cow that always used to separate from the herd. So one day he followed the cow to see where she went. There he witnessed a cobra drinking milk from her udders. That night the cowherd dreamed there was a Shiva Lingam under the ground where he had seen his cow suckling the snake. When he awoke, he went to that place and, after searching underground, he found the Shiva Lingam. Hearing of this sacred idol of worship, neighboring villagers used to go out into the field to worship there. Over time, a village grew around the Shiva Lingam. It became known as Saap, which is Marathi for "snake."

Our drive from Bombay to Saap was long and tiring, through the enormous city of Bombay, which seems to never end, and then out into the countryside, over mountainous dirt roads. Driving in India is a unique experience. It seemed that we were always just barely missing having a head-on collision with oncoming vehicles, as they squeezed by us on the narrow roads, horns honking nonstop. There were few road signs and no one seemed to follow any rules, except the tacit understanding that the bigger the vehicle, the greater the power in the kingdom of the Indian road warriors.

After seven hours of such driving, the sun began to set and

night crept in. Each time we asked Sateen, our driver, how much longer we had to go, he smiled and said, "One hour." One hour turned into several more hours. As we continued driving on back country roads in the dark, we debated whether we stop for the night. But we knew that Babu's family was waiting for us and we didn't want to disappoint them, so we kept on going. Finally, after about twelve hours of travel, exhausted and hungry, we approached Saap. Along the outskirts of the village, a few villagers, torches in hand, waved to us as if they had been expecting our arrival all day.

As soon as our road-weary entourage of three jeeps pulled into the village, loud firecrackers and sparklers went off. Men sounded long bullhorns as if announcing to all the Gods that some divine beings had finally arrived. They had been waiting for us all day long. Young boys were dancing in the streets playing cymbals and carrying a huge banner of welcome, while the rest of the townspeople clapped and danced and cheered them on, their bright, bright smiles warming our hearts and energizing our travel-weary limbs. All thoughts of the body vanished. Then, suddenly, two white oxen were led into the center of the procession, pulling a cart for Shree Maa and Swamiji to sit upon. They climbed on board and were escorted throughout the village in grand style, stopping periodically along the way for the villagers to offer them lights and offer their blessings. The entire village had gathered to greet Shree Maa, Swamiji and the rest of us.

The ox cart drove right to the entrance of the residence where we would be staying. From the outside it looked like just like the royal fortress it once had been, with massive wooden doors studded with pointed metal barbs to keep off attacking elephants in earlier times. The doors were flung open, and we dismounted. After more dancing and celebration, we proceeded slowly into the courtyard and up a few stairs to a huge veranda, where Shree Maa and Swamiji sat in two chairs to offer blessings to all who came. One by one all the people of the town came to them and bowed down. There must have been over 800 people. Swamiji distributed chocolate to them all.

The next day, as is their habit, Shree Maa and Swamiji arose early and performed Shiva Puja in one of the courtyards. We spent the day visiting and worshipping in Saap's temples. The following day was particularly auspicious for the Goddess Kali, so a Kali Puja was performed and preparations were made for a big Kali homa. Swamiji prepared a havan kund in one of the courtyards. That night the sacred fire blazed brilliantly as we all chanted the thousand names of Mahakali, lighting up the hearts and minds of the villagers who came to worship with us. After the homa was completed, we learned that for the first time in hundreds of years, there was peace in this ancient palace. Babu's father told us that many souls who had lived there a long time ago had been trapped between this world and the next, and with the fire ceremony their souls were released. They were extremely happy now and the palace once more had peace.

The next day was Diwali, the festival of lights. We sang the *Sundar Kanda* and made preparations to feed the entire village. Many of the women of the village came and helped us prepare the vegetables and make over two thousand chapatis. As night fell, the village elders entered the grand house to pay their respects. We enjoyed feeding them. As the evening continued, more and more villagers came, arriving in groups of twenty or more, until by the end of the evening we had fed a thousand people. After the meal, there was again celebration — dancing and singing together in happiness, knowing in our hearts that we were all brothers and sisters connected by the one Supreme Divinity manifest in all objects of creation. It had been over one hundred and fifty years since Diwali had been celebrated in the village of Saap. So, once again, Swamiji and Maa had brought the hearts and minds of the people back to the celebratory worship of God.

Swamiji does not teach one spiritual technique to incorporate into life, but rather, like Shree Maa, lives a deeply spiritual way of life, and teaches through his example. His concept of spiritual life is one in which we give more than we take and add value to other peoples' lives. As the *Devi Gita* says, "Each moment is a festival." Each breath we take is a cause to celebrate. Each breath is another chance to remember God. It is in this way that Swamiji lives and inspires others to do the same. May anyone who reads this book be inspired to search for and realize the highest goal of existence. Peace in the heavens, peace on the earth, peace within and peace beyond.

Gautam's Story

Swami Satyananda has said over the years that the true spiritual aspirant gathers together all the loose threads of his or her life in order to focus on the goals and methods to reach them. "To be a true sadhu is to be efficient, and to give more than one takes." Looking over the sixteen years I have known them, I can recall examples of Mother's and Swamiji's one-pointedness, their simplicity in facing both social and financial crises with calm, their wisdom and spiritual dexterity, all to a degree worthy of the highest saints.

One time when we ran out of flowers for puja, Swamiji told us about the times in India when he had no flowers for puja. He would simply use the leaves of trees, offering them in orderly and artistic patterns with the accompanying mantras. He does the same in United States when necessary.

Once we had just rented a house in the back hills of Moraga, behind Saint Mary's College in the San Francisco Bay Area. A few devotees were assisting in building our havan kund, a pit for containing the sacred fire. I took off work early one day to help with the construction. As I came up the driveway, I looked over at the structure and saw Swamiji on his knees in the wet soil, forming the beginnings of our first sacrificial fire pit. He was so engrossed in placing the bricks and covering them with mud and cow dung, that he did not notice me. I walked up with wonder, grateful for the privilege of being in his company, as he smeared the muddy plaster over the bricks with his hands. I thought, "Here indeed is a man who is in love with God."

His face was alight as he looked up and said, "This is our first havan kund."

After we had finished the superstructure of the fire pit, we covered it Indian-style with corrugated metal to ensure that the rain would not come in. We gathered together many cardboard boxes to make walls for protection against strong gusts of wind.

Another time, while worshipping at the fire, we determinedly kept our asanas as the wind violently tore through the cardboard walls and whipped up the sacrificial fire while we were chanting the *Chandi*. The wind spread smoke and sparks every which way. I saw that Mother and Swamiji were solid in their commitment to their vows of worship and would not be shaken by a mere storm. They did not move from their asanas until the recitation was completed.

Swamiji is an open channel for receiving divine grace. Whoever is fortunate enough to be open to the divine flow will undoubtedly receive it. It remains up to us to direct the gift toward changing our own lives and sharing our love with all the people we meet.

While at the Moraga house, Shree Maa, Swamiji and some devotees went on a ten day camping retreat to Panther Meadows at Mount Shasta. We lived there as they had lived in India. We would get up early before dawn, perform group puja before a wilderness Shiva Puja altar and then have a campfire breakfast. Swamiji sat for the *Chandi* from seven in the morning to seven in the evening. He chanted the *Chandi* with the Navarna Mantra (the principal mantra of *Chandi*) repeated before and after each verse in the method called *Samput*. After completing the *Chandi* from the front to the back, he would then chant it from the back to the

front with the same weaving of the Navarna Mantra into his recitation. He did this seven times in one asana for twelve hours. I
thought to myself, "How he loves to be one with the Divine Mother
in continuous praise of her victorious battle with the ego!"

At the same retreat Swamiji and I were offering the Shiva
mantra at the homa late one night. I thought I heard a distinct but
soft humming sound come down from above, perhaps from the
trees. Asking Swamiji about this, he replied, "Yes, the trees are
singing, *Om Namah Shivaya* because they are happy with the
sadhana we are performing here. Prakriti and Purush are dancing
in harmony with each other, giving birth to the Consciousness of
Infinite Goodness!"

Over the years I have had the opportunity to be at many of
Swamiji's classes. The classes have ranged in subject from a hands-
on instruction on how to build a havan kund with mud and cow
dung plaster, to how Socrates won debates with sophisticated con-
temporaries, to classes on Sanskrit grammar and pronunciation
and philosophy. He has also given instruction on the inner meanings of the many books he has written.

On a High Sierra Retreat with Swamiji and many brother disciples in 1997, I had the opportunity to relax and look inward for
ten days. It was a wonder to have the privilege of being with
Swamiji and fellow seekers. We were learning the way to synthesize spiritual concepts with actual practice in a natural setting.
We came to a height of 9500 feet in order to concentrate on our
sadhana, and to absorb Swamiji's teachings under the trees and
meditate near the lake.

Since I first met Swamiji in 1984, he has been a steady, efficient guide in the practical matters of daily life as well as in age-

less spiritual truths. He emphasizes that one can strive to synthesize the teaching of the rishis with one's immediate concerns, aspirations and situations. Swamiji shows us how to weave (which is the real meaning of the word tantra) these teachings in order to live every moment of life in bhava, the pure intuitive actualization of infinite love.

I will close with just one example of how his teachings affected my understanding. When we were in the High Sierras, some of the younger devotees had seen Swamiji sitting naked on the snow chanting the *Chandi*. He did not insist that anyone try this method, but some of us were inspired to do so. On four different occasions, I walked away from the group down to a hidden ice bank ravine beside a snow-fed stream. I told myself I was doing this not to compete with anyone but just to put a little more effort into my sadhana. Mother gives us the freedom to create an atmosphere of surrender for ourselves. It is something like a self-test. I went back and asked Swamiji about my doing the tapasya after my first or second attempt.

He replied, "You don't need to worry about sitting on the ice and chanting. Leave this to the younger people. Your goal is to concentrate on your sadhana and to just improve on what you've been given already. It is not to sit on the ice chanting. Don't ruin your body. You should try to integrate the sadhana that you have already learned with love, and radiate the bhava by supporting all the younger disciples who are eager to learn. Don't let the fact that they are doing certain disciplines challenge you to go to the extreme. Just maintain your bhava all the time."

Two days later, I was going back to my tent to rest after chanting on the ice a couple of times. I saw Swamiji and went over to ask him the same question he had already answered. I asked, "Swamiji, how is sitting on the ice and chanting going to help anyone get into the bhava of love and remain there?"

The answer came swiftly, "Sitting on the ice isn't your sadhana now. You have to be in love and radiate love. You have to be in bhava all the time and give encouragement to these young people. They have a great desire for God and the focus to leave all else to be here at the Devi Mandir. Don't try acting like them. The sadhana I practiced while chanting on ice came after I had learned the meanings of the mantras. After learning much Sanskrit, grammar and pronunciation, I could undertake the more advanced disciplines. You haven't perfected the elementary practices yet. Why are you striving to practice the advanced techniques when you haven't completed the elementary training? Stay on the land, chant and learn, not on the ice. I chanted on the ice to gain a specific siddhi in chanting. It was not to prove that I could do it. Chant and perfect your pronunciation and understanding on land and be in bhava before you become concerned with sitting on the ice."

I asked, "Yes, but isn't it true that age is a mental concept, no matter how old your physical body is? Is it better not to accept age as a barrier to trying to sit on the ice?"

Swamiji replied, "The soul is eternal, but your body is sixty years old. Just be in the bhava and radiate love. Chant on the land while perfecting your pronunciation and learning of Sanskrit without ruining your health."

Even after this conversation, I spent one more session chanting on the ice. When I finished chanting the Thousand Names of Shiva, I noticed as I arose from the asana that part of my left calf muscle and foot had turned blue. As I desperately massaged my feet to regain blood circulation, I thought over my discussion with Swamiji again. I recalled the old saying, "Night seems darkest right before the dawn." I quietly and slowly walked up the steep snow slope toward the camp, favoring my right leg.

Swamiji smiled as I walked past his tent and inquired about my chanting. I said, "All was well," even knowing that it was not. I gratefully went to my tent to rest, smiling inwardly about the little test that ultimately did not prove anything. I thank Swamiji for giving the remedy to save the patient, even when the patient did not want to swallow the pill. Learning Sanskrit and practicing pronunciation, especially on dry land, never looked so good as it does from the perspective I have today!

Swamiji sitting on the ice in prayer

Uma's Interview: Riding the Caravan of Peace

In the humid midsummer heat of upstate New York, a fire ceremony couldn't sound less appealing. Yet here was a man, dressed all in orange, sitting in front of a huge fire and chanting hymns of praise to the ancient Indian Goddess in a tantalizing voice, with an impeccable pronunciation of the Sanskrit language, and making the fire itself sweat.

When seeing Swami Satyananda dive into the animated fire with generous offerings of rice, sesame seeds, barley and clarified butter to invoke the divine presence, thoughts of creature comforts become replaced with the longing for a glimpse of the Goddess. I felt a rush of energy and lightness overwhelm my body, and there I was smiling, not really knowing why. Then the circle around the ceremonial fire started singing beautiful songs led by a very silent and still woman with a mystically melodious voice, Shree Maa. As their voices became more and more ecstatic, and the music grew wild, I found myself dancing around, filled with energy, even after 12 hours of cooking for an entire ashram. Next thing I knew, I was riding in a modest RV across the country with a saint from India by the name of Shree Maa and Swami Satyananda.

I've always enjoyed spontaneous adventures, but I must admit this was the most intriguing and mystical one I had ever stumbled upon. As the wide hills and valleys of the United States led our caravan to Shree Maa's sanctuary in Napa, California, I was led through the perils of my own heart and asked the most important questions in my life. My adventure lasted a month and a half, but the impact seems eternal.

I am in New York City now, so I decided to contact Swami Satyananda and ask him a few questions about the lifestyle I have chosen to embrace.

Q. What is Hinduism?

A. Hinduism is an evolving theology. It's more of a way of life than a codified religion. So in Hinduism you'll find staunch agnostics, you'll find materialists, you'll find idealists and everything in between. They're all Hindu because of a specific lifestyle.

Q. And what is the lifestyle?

A. The definition of a Hindu is "He who abhors violence in every form, who strives for harmony in every behavior, who loves wisdom, who respects all teachers of wisdom, who practices one-pointed meditation – such a person may be called a Hindu."

Q. You mentioned different philosophical perspectives within Hinduism, what is the unifying link?

A. Traditionally the common link has been the respect of the Vedas. Vedas are a body of wisdom, which is to be known by all individuals, and it is known only through intense spiritual practices. So all the groups of Hindus rely on the authority of the Vedas.

Q. The Vedas being the main scriptures of Hinduism…

A. Certainly they are the oldest of the scriptures. Therefore, all the more modern scriptures refer back to the Vedas. Each of the more modern scriptures attempts to update or restate the position of the Vedas in the vernacular of the current time.

Q. Like the amendments to the Constitution?

A. No, not necessarily. I think they are reaffirmations of the Vedas. They are the translations of the Vedas into the language of today.

Q. Can we create new reaffirmations of the Vedas for the current society?

A. Absolutely, we are doing it right now. I have written about two dozen books that trace their heritage, lineage and all the information within them back to the Vedas.

Q. Eastern spirituality, Yoga in particular, has become extremely popular in the West. What is the explanation for this phenomenon? Are we disillusioned with our own religions?

A. Eastern spirituality places the emphasis on the individual to pursue his or her own path of spirituality, to find his or her own balance, so it's based more on a personal experience. The western religious heritage, in contrast, is based more on a congregational approach. So when we go to a church or a synagogue, we find that the congregation is facing an altar and there is individual who is interceding in the congregation's relationship with God.

Q. I see. He is like a middleman; there is no direct relationship.

A. Yes. When you go to a Hindu ceremony, everyone faces the altar and everyone participates in exploring his or her own relationship with God.

Q. In America, especially, people are drawn to define their individuality. Maybe that's why eastern spirituality makes more sense.

A. Certainly, also there are many concepts that are relevant to the American individual. Holistic health, for example. We all see how the health system as it stands today has really failed the population. In fact it was Tulsidas who said when doctors, lawyers and other intimate counselors are the highest paid members of society, then justice, health and good common sense become servants of wealth. It is important that this doesn't happen, so that the objective is to maintain good health, justice and fairness for all. Ayurvedic diet and medicine, and Yoga, are attempts to democratize health, diet, good body physique and posture so that the individual can have a personal relationship with divinity. A diseased body can only pray to God for relief from disease, but a healthy body can pray for relief from all emotional distress.

Q. You just touched upon the issue of distress or suffering. Suffering exists beyond the personal, especially today, considering the violent calamities in the Middle East, the Balkans and other politically vulnerable places. How is eastern spirituality relevant to the politics around us and the elimination of suffering?

A. Well, it was Confucius who said that it was impossible to have a peaceful nation unless we have a peaceful state, and we can't have peaceful states until we have peaceful families, and we can't have peaceful families until we have individuals who are in harmony with themselves. So here eastern spirituality places the responsibility for peace among nations on every individual. We are responsible for the type of environment we live in, and we can improve our environment by creating peace within ourselves, our families, communities, etc.

Q. So it doesn't really offer any immediate relief from massive suffering?

A. Massive suffering has existed from the beginning of humanity, from the beginning of time, and can't be alleviated in one generation. But what we can hope to do is, by being examples ourselves of individuals in harmony, we can create inspiration in our communities for more people to join the harmony. And as we do that, we'll find fewer people attracted to violence and more people attracted to harmony.

Q. How do you spread this harmony?

A. Shree Maa, myself and others in our community spread harmony around by going to communities around the world and reaching out to them by putting on programs of inspiration through music, dance and spiritual ceremonies. When asked, we teach people how to do the same in the temples of their own homes and thus to create an environment conducive to peace and harmony for themselves and their families.

Q. Who in turn will take that peace to communities, states and nations, and complete the formula of Confucius?

A. That's right.

Q. You mentioned Shree Maa. Who is she?

A. Shree Maa is a saint from North India. She is a teacher of spirituality and an example who inspires thousands of people around the world. Her name means the respected Holy Mother, and she is a teacher in the lineage of Sri Ramakrishna, a nineteenth century saint, who taught that all paths are a means of attaining union with the divine. He taught that there shouldn't be any religious disharmony because all paths are translations of the one truth into the native languages of the religion. Shree Maa is teaching and demonstrating that no caste, creed or religious sectarianism will be an asset in getting us into a greater position of harmony. We have to abandon all kinds of limitations in order to move towards a greater harmony and peace.

Q. The role of women has been really controversial in religions. How do you explain Shree Maa's gender and her position in the congregation?

A. You'll find in the Hindu pantheon of Divine beings an

equal number of Goddesses as the number of Gods. God herself is neither masculine nor feminine, but we relate to him or her according to our tradition or understanding. Generally when we think of the female aspects of divinity we think of the nourishing capacity, the capacity that can bring a new birth and nurture creation. When we relate to divinity in the form of the Divine Mother, we put away all violence and move towards a greater harmony. We think of how to nourish, nurture, inspire, instruct and work for the common unity. We think of the Divine Mother as Goddess Saraswati, who'll give us the knowledge and understanding of how to find our way. We think of Goddess Laxmi, who defines our path, and we think of Goddess Kali, who takes away our darkness. We think of her as the Goddess Durga, who removes our difficulties and obstructions, and we think of her as compassionate Shree Maa, who is always working for the benefit of her congregation, just like a mother nourishing her family.

Q. If you were to sum up the goals of spiritual life, would they be unity and harmony?

A. That's very good. I'd also add love and respect. There is a place in that unity where all the positive qualties unite: love, joy, wisdom, peace, respect, worship — they are all one.

Mahavir's Story

One morning in Pushkar, India, Swamiji and I were walking back from a session of singing by the banks of a beautiful lake. We took our usual path through the town that led back to our humble dharmsala, where we were staying. I was feeling light and playful, and was once again struck by the incredible incongruity of being in India, which is an experience not unlike landing on another planet. It defies description or explanation. Here I was, dressed in Indian clothes, walking through a colorful, chaotic street alongside this Swami in orange robes. This nice, middle-class Jewish boy, who was taught to be careful of strangers, is walking in one of the strangest places on earth. I couldn't contain myself any longer. I exultantly cried to Swami, "If my mother could see me now!"

Instantly, Swami pointed his finger to a building on our left and said, "Look!" Unbelievably, there was Hebrew writing on the wall. Then Swami pointed to the right, where I saw a sign that was also written in Hebrew. The very next moment a man walked by with a T-shirt that had the star of David and the word "Israel" printed on it. It was so strange, like we had entered a Jewish universe. I had never seen anything like it in my six trips to India, and it just happened to occur at that very moment.

That's typical of what it's like to hang out with Swamiji. It's unpredictable, unlikely and a lot of fun. You never know what is going to happen next. Just saying "hello" to Swami can be a memorable experience. Often when he sees someone he says in a loud, jubilant voice, "Boy am I glad to see you!" Then he comes up really close and hugs you, or jokes with you, and asks you how you are. You can't help but feel immediately involved with him. He's so engaging there's no place else you want to go.

Swami loves to play and I enjoy playing along with him. Sometimes he'll pretend to be mad at me and say that he has a "bone to pick with me." As he walks closer, I pretend that I am afraid of him. He moves forward and I move back. Once he chased me around the temple. Sometimes he comes nose to nose and points his finger in my chest in mock anger. It's hilarious and just the kind of fun you had when you were a kid.

There was one greeting with Swamiji I will never forget. One morning I greeted him with a "Namaste" and bowed to him slightly with my hands in prayer position, the traditional Namaste gesture. Swamiji responded with a deeper bow that was closer to the ground. I returned an even deeper bow. Before I knew it, this Swami dove all the way to the ground and stretched out in a full bow or pranam posture. I quickly followed suit and we were both lying on the ground facing each other. Then he grasped my hands and we held each others' hands and laughed. How many spiritual teachers would do that?

Swami's office is presently a small trailer with a number of computers arrayed before him. He sits on the floor. It's always a pleasure to spend time in his little office. Whether he is singing his e-mails or talking to his computers or joking with you, Swami is in perpetual, purposeful motion. He demonstrates how to work for God in a joyful way that is infectious. One thing is certain, you are not going to fall asleep around this man. He is constantly drawing you into his joyous spirit.

Swami is so down to earth and unpretentious that he won't let himself get stuck in a "holy man" role. In fact, he is constantly breaking the rules about how an enlightened teacher should act. In the Tibetan tradition this is called "crazy wisdom," a quality that many great masters possess. Since Swami is breaking the rules all the time, you never know what is going to happen next when you're with him and thus spontaneity and gaiety always surround him.

Swami is also willing to make fun of himself and to have fun with himself. His spontaneous behavior allows you to feel comfortable with him. He makes you feel like you are on the same level as he. He allows you to be yourself and not take yourself too seriously. Shree Maa says that this ability is a mark of his greatness. He is so great that he can hide his power so he won't intimidate us. To me Swami demonstrates one of the most unique teaching roles: the spiritual teacher as a true friend.

Letters and E-mails

Following are some of the many e-mails and letters that Swamiji and Shree Maa receive daily. We have included them to give a taste of what it is like to attend a program or class with them, to read their books, to listen to their CDs and, most importantly, to worship, chant, sing and dance the praises of the Divine in life as they have taught.

Most beloved Shree Maa and Swamiji:
I attended a gathering which was graced by your presence in St. Louis, Missouri at the home of Jimmy and Janice Eyerman. My heart is still filled with the joy and love we shared that evening. You both are truly divine spirits! I have been graced with the capacity to love at the deepest level all that comes into my life. Each interaction I experience is a true gift from God. My heart is full of the joy that the universe has provided me. Thank you for traveling to our city and spending the time that you did with us! We are all still talking about you and sharing in the love that you helped us to generate those few days that you were here. I am embarking on a journey through nursing school and am devoting my life to the healing of children. I would appreciate any blessing that you might bestow upon me to add to the loving energy that will fuel my path to complete God's work in my life. God bless you both for the joy you bring to our hearts! Namaste!
jd

Dearest Shree Maa and Swamiji
I'll start out by echoing Indrani's sentiments regarding the day you entered into our lives. So much love, so many blessings in such a short space of time. Our lives are turned around....like small plants reaching out for the sun in whatever direction it moves....we turn to you to feed us so that we can grow by your grace in your light. Words are not enough.... We love you and we feel that love growing with each moment. Thank you for welcoming us into the family!!
dr

Swamiji,
Hope your tour is going well. Looks like you will soon be going home. I was so touched by Maa and you during your visit here in Minnesota... how can I keep up the blissful feelings inside? What practices do you recommend? Should one recite the Durga mantra? The *Chandi*? I wonder what to do next. Any help you could provide would be great. Thank you for coming here!
kb

Dear Shree Maa,
Your Swamiji is so utterly delightful. I have listened to his stories on the CD, and it makes me feel like he is right there with me in the car. And having his voice with me fills me with joy and happiness. The story of the king and the cut finger helps me be not so impatient to sell my practice and join you. I know it is all working out all right. With all my love to you and Swami,
sk

Dear Swamiji,
Thank you and thank you for all you and Shree Maa did for Vicki. What blessed times we live in. With love from all of us,
mb

Rev Swamiji,
Thank you very much for allowing me to stay overnight at the Devi Mandir. I am really thankful for your cordiality and warmth. It was very enjoyable and soul searching. Simplicity in living makes one realize the difference between what one needs and what one wants to have. Devi Mandir filled me with love and gratitude. With great respect and love
vg

Dearest Mother and Father,
Thank you for the time you spent with us in Atlanta. Thank you for your exquisite example/role model for sadhana/sat sang, for your LOVE, determination and single-mindedness. We received great inspiration, blessings and healing from you both. I love your tapes and books. Your way captures my heart — it is my heart's desire to be so simple, so pure, so fearless in KNOWING-LOVING-SERVING God in absolute surrender and devotion! By His/Her grace it is done.
lw

Dear Shree Maa and Swamiji,

Jai Maa! Thank you for coming to Fairfield and Blessing our town with Happiness, Love and Devotion (and more!). You inspire us to be more attentive to God and to share His love with everyone. We are eager to be with you in your next program.

Namaste,

sm

Dear Swamiji,

My friends and I were at the Chicago and Iowa programs, and I just want to let you know that we enjoyed it so very much and feel that we benefitted by being with you and Shree Maa. We don't know what we ever did to be lucky enough to have such association, but we're glad we did.

Peace & Blessing,

pp

Dear Shree Maa & Swamiji,

Enjoyed spending the weekend with you in New York on Mother's Day Weekend. My girlfriend & I were the ones who greeted you early in the morning on Mother's Day Sunday on the road outside the temple. Maa wished us a Happy Mother's Day. You have both had a tremendous impact on my life. Your examples of devotion and the pure energy of your presence are still with me. Marsha and I have started chanting the 1000 names of Kali along with Maa's CD, and it has a profound effect on both of us. We will never forget when Maa said, "Nobody is separate from me." We were both struck by lightning bolts simultaneously as she said it. We get it!! I want to order your CD about the Sadhu Stories. We think Swamiji is an excellent teacher. I want to know what kind of vitamins he takes. I want some of that boundless energy he displays. Is it all from worship or is there some secret Sadhu potion I should know about? Please advise.

Please add me to your e-mail list for your activities or anything else you would like to communicate. Thanks for the Shakti, Love,

eg

Dear Maa and Swamiji,
Namaste! What a blessing it was to be with you. I feel renewed
energy and clarity of purpose after that wonderful purification, and so
grateful that somehow I was allowed to come into contact with you and
receive your divine glance and blessings. Thanks again and again. Love
to everyone.
mb

Swamiji,
What a great four days with you and Maa. I want you to know you
were brilliant. That program was masterfully presented and your energy
and skill with the precious child Goddess was the the best I've ever
seen. That was a difficult and prolonged event that you made look ef-
fortless. Again, we leave with much more than we came with, things
that words can't describe.
Thank you from all of my heart.
tw

Dear Shree Maa and Swamiji,
I just wanted to tell you both how wonderful it is to be in your Presence. I know I am so blessed. I find it difficult to believe. I guess I have
been preparing for this for many lifetimes. It is good to finally get here. It
has been a long road. I'm glad I can't remember.
Well, I love you two. As a matter of fact I had lunch today in a res-
taurant and, who was sitting there, but a devotee I met the other night.
So we talked about you and Shree Maa the whole time, and shared our
totally blissed out experiences with you two unbelievable, fantastic,
delicious beings from who knows where. Jai Maa
sm

Dear Shree Maa and Swamiji,
We want you to know that we appreciated our weekend together
very very very much. We are honored to be present with you all. We
appreciate your great LOVE and sharing. The magic and wonder that is
your life message is utterly beyond any recordable human expression.
We were welcomed into your family with such ease and gracious love.
We are yours forever and gratefully you are ours. In LOVE.
nm

Respected Swamiji,
This is just a note of appreciation and gratitude from a Devi-bhakta who has recently purchased your book *Chandi Path*. I come from a family of Bhagavathy worshippers, and from a young age have been reading the *Devi Mahatmyam* (as it is called in Kerala) and also chanting *Lalitha Sahasranamam*. But your book has given me a lot of new insights and I'm using it for my daily worship now.
I live in India and the distance prevents me from actively involving myself in Devi Mandir activities; and if the travel costs hadn't been so prohibitive, I would have definitely offered my services to the Mandir and personally offered pranams to Shree Maa and Swamiji. Please aceept my grateful pranams through this letter,
dv, Kerala

Dear Shree Maa and Swamiji and the Devi Mandir Family,
Please accept my love and salutations on this Guru Purnima evening. There are no words to express my profound gratefulness for all that you have given to me and my spiritual family over the past few years. May the Light of wisdom, truth and service blaze in my heart forever in recognition of your Love. You have helped me recognize the Inner Guru and the reality of pure love. These gifts are of the greatest merit. Jai Ramakrishna, Jai Jesus, Jai Maa. All my love and respect,
jl

Dear Swamiji,
Maa has stated that you are her Guru. So therefore you are my Paramaguru. Please forgive me for not showing you the appropriate respect. You are both on my mind and in my heart always! I feel like a gnat bothering you constantly. I cannot help myself in writing as much as I do. Please forgive me, I am only a bug (my favorite line from the movie "Kundun"). Knowing as I do that every bug is a manifestation of the Supreme Lord. To just think of you both brings tears of joy to this jiva.
rt

Shree Maa
walked into the temple
with Swamiji at her side
at the site of them there
oh how my soul cried

Maa
walked straight up to me
my dreams standing so near
looked deep into my soul
she said "you brought me here"

Kali
I have prayed for this day
to meet you face to face
to fall at your feet
and bathe in your Grace

Shree Maa
has conquered our hearts
she has lifted our souls
brought me to my knees
joyessness untold.

Swamiji
has brightened the way
the smile on his face
he is the Vedas voice
the blessings unfold

Homa Fire
Hanuman does abide
at Swamiji's side
Maa feeds the fire
Our every desire

with Love and Devotion;
ja

Sending love and light out to Shree Maa and Swamiji.
Thank you for the love and beauty that you send out to the world; may your blessings allow everyone to one day see the light and embrace it. Hopefully, one day soon. May your loving thoughts be with me at all times, and be with all my fellow creatures. Thinking of you and wishing you all the love in the world. Best wishes,
sf, UK

Shree Maa and Swamiji,
I attended your evening program held at the Friends Meetinghouse in Cambridge, MA. First of all, Shree Maa, you are the most beautiful woman I have ever beheld. Thank you for the privilege of seeing you. Secondly, I immensely enjoyed the bhajans, the spirit, Swamiji's expressiveness and impulsive joy, and the genuine heartfelt welcome you extended to who all came. In many respects it was a revelation. I look forward to attending one of your 9 day pujas. Sincerely,
mo, Paris

My Beloved Mother and Dearest Swamiji,
Thank you both from the bottom of my heart for opening the *Chandi* to me. You have given me a great treasure that shall guide me through the rest of my life and my future incarnations. I love you both more than words can express. You are both a fountain of spirituality that has sustained this jiva. With Love and Devotion,
ja

Dear Shree Maa & Swamiji,
Thank you for the 3 wonderful days you gave us in Copenhagen. We just fell in love with you, and hope for your return. Please e-mail me about your activities and tours. Love from a great fan of yours.
kw, Copenhagen

Namaste... namaste.
The Swamiji from the Vedanta Society called me today, as he is so excited about having found You. He has chanted the whole *Chandi* every day for years. He said — Your books are translated with "so much inner understanding" and they can be chanted — the type is large enough. He never met anyone who respected the *Chandi Path* as much as you do. He can't wait to meet You and Maa.
hh

Notes

[1] White holy man

[2] Seat for meditation or worship

[3] Wandering holy men

[4] Mixture of Indian spices

[5] Ceremony for worship of the gods and goddesses involving making offerings of food, flowers, scents, cloth, etc.

[6] Ceremony of worship of the gods and goddesses involving offering light, playing instruments, singing their praises, and dancing ecstatically

[7] The nectar of immortal bliss

[8] Purifying austerities of one-pointed worship

[9] A homa is a short fire ceremony, lasting anywhere from an hour or two to an entire day. A yagya is a longer fire ceremony, lasting anywhere from a few days to years.

[10] Part of the sadhu's vow was to never cut his hair

[11] Bakranath means the Lord of the infirm

[12] Victory to the great teacher, Satyananda

[13] Ganges River

[14] Literally, disease of the gods, a common name for leprosy

[15] The Naxalite Movement was an attempt by the lawless poor to terrorize the rich.

[16] A yagya vedi is an altar for the fire sacrifice upon which the fire is enkindled.

[17] A special worship for the Goddess of Wealth

[18] A brahmacharya is one who has vowed to move with God.

[19] A ceremonial lamp which holds lighted wicks which are waved before the deities.

[20] Blessed food that has been offered to the gods and goddesses

[21] Blessed vision

[22] The priests of the famous temple

[23] Demon

[24] The territory of Gaya. A kshetra is a field or area.

[25] Actions not in harmony with divine law

[26] Dark half of the lunar cycle

[27] Priest

[28] Literaly, communion with truth. A spiritual gathering for sharing fellowship and knowledge.

[29] Someone who is practicing the eternal ideals of perfection

[30] Literally, "Respected Mother." An endearing term indicating a much beloved, spiritual motherly figure.

[31] Thin piece of cloth with assorted uses, e.g., as a towel, handkerchief, to cover oneself while bathing in public, etc.

[32] A special puja to the Divine Mother in the form of Chandi in which all the deities mentioned in the *Chandi Path* are worshipped.

[33] One of Lakshmi's aspects is as the Goddess of Wealth. It is common to pray to Lakshmi for success in financial matters, although for sadhus, like Swamiji, who have given up their material attachments, prayers to Lakshmi are more often made for the attainment or fulfillment of their goals.

[34] Thief or violent man.

[35] The hymn to the Ganges which says, "O Supreme Goddess above the Gods, O Ganga whose waters nourish the three worlds..."

[36] Victory to Mother Ganga!

[37] Nava means nine and ratri means nights. The Navaratri is the vow of worship for the Divine Mother lasting nine days and nine nights.

[38] The temporary structure which housed the temple.

[39] A style of chanting where we weave one mantra between the other mantras throughout the text.

[40] Revered mother

[41] Female sadhu

[42] Vow of worship

[43] Rickshaw driver

[44] The clay idol of worship

[45] Dissolving the clay deity in the rive

[46] A blessing of ashes applied to the third eye-

Books by Shree Maa and Swami Satyananda Saraswati

Annapurna Sahasranam
Before Becoming This
Bhagavad Gita
Chandi Path
Cosmic Puja
Devi Gita
Devi Mandir Songbook
Durga Puja Beginner
Ganesh Puja
Hanuman Puja
Kali Dhyanam
Kali Puja
Shiva Puja Beginner
Shiva Puja and Advanced Yajna
Shree Maa Cookbook
Shree Maa: The Guru and the Goddess
Shree Maa: The Life of a Saint
Sundar Kanda
Swami Purana

CDs and Cassettes

Chandi Path
Dark Night Mother
Goddess is Everywhere
Lalita Trishati
Mahamrtyunjaya Mantra
Navarna Mantra
Om Mantra
Sadhu Stories from the Himalayas

Shiva is in My Heart
Shiva Puja Beginner (Instructional)
Shiva Puja & Advanced Yajna
Shree Maa in the Temple of the Heart
Shree Maa on Tour 1998
Songs of Ramprasad
Thousand Names of Kali

Videos

Across the States with Shree Maa & Swamiji
Meaning and Method of Worship
Shree Maa: Meeting a Modern Saint
Visiting India with Shree Maa and Swamiji

Please visit us at www.shreemaa.org
Our email is info@shreemaa.org